CHASING IMMORTALITY

The Science, Ethics, and Dreams of Living Forever

Pranav Pandya

INDIA · SINGAPORE · MALAYSIA

ISBN
Paperback 979-8-89673-365-2
Hardcase 979-8-89724-932-9

Author's Note

Dear Reader,

I've always believed that the most profound truths are found in simplicity. Growing up in India, I was surrounded by the timeless wisdom of ancient texts and spiritual practices like yoga. These teachings weren't just concepts to be studied; they were ways of living. Yoga, meditation, and philosophies like Vedanta taught me to embrace life's impermanence — to live with balance, meaning, and a sense of connection to something eternal within us all. They taught me that while the body is temporary, there is something within each of us that goes beyond time.

It's probably no surprise, then, that the idea of living forever has always fascinated me. For many ancient traditions, living forever was never about living forever in a physical sense. Instead, it was about transcending the body, finding union with the divine, or realizing the soul's infinite nature. But as I started exploring the modern world's quest for living forever, I was struck by how different it was. No longer just a spiritual pursuit, today's search for living forever is driven by science and technology. Billionaires, scientists, and futurists are now racing to conquer death itself — not through inner transformation but through external innovation.

This contrast, between ancient wisdom and modern ambition, became the inspiration for Chasing Immortality: The Science, Ethics, and Dreams of Living Forever. This book is my attempt to explore this fascinating and intriguing pursuit of eternal life. It's a journey that spans the fields of biotechnology, artificial intelligence (AI), and regenerative medicine.

But the more I researched, the more I realized that this isn't just about trying to "cheat death." It's about something much deeper: the human desire to transcend limits. In many ways, it's the same desire that ancient yogis have pursued for centuries, but with one crucial difference — where the ancients looked within, today's visionaries are looking outward.

This book is also a reflection of my journey as an entrepreneur and writer. Over the years, I've explored how we can overcome challenges, improve productivity, and live in harmony with ourselves and the world around us. In my first book, Overcoming Adversity: Inspiring Stories of Resilience and Triumph, I shared real stories of people who faced incredible challenges and still found a way to rise. Those stories taught me that human beings are incredibly adaptable and resilient. And that same spirit of resilience — the drive to overcome, to push past limits — is at the heart of humanity's quest for living forever.

In Mindful Productivity, I explored how mindfulness could help us slow down, focus, and lead more intentional lives. I wanted to show how ancient practices could guide us in a fast-paced world. It was a way of grounding ourselves in the present moment, something I think is more important than ever as we race toward an uncertain future.

Then came Mind-Body Mastery, a book that focused on the powerful connection between mind and body. Practices like yoga and meditation aren't just spiritual tools; they're ways to improve physical and mental well-being. This idea of "mastering" the mind-body connection became central to my thinking about living forever.

After all, if we can learn to master the mind and body, are we not, in some sense, already on the path to transcendence?

But Chasing Immortality takes things a step further. Here, I'm not just exploring self-mastery; I'm looking at how we, as a society, are trying to master life itself. With advances in genetic engineering, stem cell research, and regenerative medicine, we're witnessing breakthroughs that could redefine aging. Technologies like AI and machine learning are driving research forward at a pace we've never seen before. Some believe that one day, we'll be able to "upload" our consciousness into the cloud, achieving a form of digital living forever.

This brings me to something that fascinates me on a deeply personal level: the influence of AI on the human psyche. We often talk about AI as if it's just a tool, something that helps us make faster decisions or offers us better recommendations. But I believe it's more than that. As we rely on AI to think, predict, and create for us, we're subtly reshaping our perception of reality. We may even be altering our sense of what it means to be "alive." What happens when a machine can outlive us? What happens when a machine can predict our choices before we make them? How does this affect our idea of self, soul, and legacy?

This topic felt so significant that I dedicated an entire chapter to it in this book. I explore how AI isn't just affecting the "how" of living forever but also the "why." If we become more dependent on machines to think for us, are we still fully human? If we upload our consciousness into a digital space, are we still "us"? Or have we become something else entirely?

These are big questions, and I don't pretend to have all the answers. But as I researched and wrote this book, I realized that this pursuit of living forever — whether technological or spiritual — is not just about extending life. It's about the search for meaning. We chase living forever because we want to leave something behind, to make an impact, to ensure that some part of us continues. And perhaps, that is what unites both the spiritual seekers of old and the scientists of today.

So as you read this book, I invite you to reflect on your own relationship with life and death. What would it mean to you to live forever? Would it be a blessing or a burden? Is it better to chase longevity, or to chase purpose? My hope is that this book will spark new thoughts, deeper questions, and moments of reflection.

At its heart, this book is a conversation, a bridge between the ancient wisdom that has guided me and the modern marvels that are reshaping our world. It's a reflection of my own journey as a student of life, as a believer in spiritual growth, and as a seeker of truth. I'm incredibly grateful that you've chosen to join me on this journey.

Thank you for being here. I hope this book inspires you to think, reflect, and maybe even challenge your own ideas about life, death, and everything in between.

Warmly,

Pranav Pandya

Table of Contents

The Role of Death in Giving Life Meaning: Does Immortality Diminish Value?

A critical examination of whether the absence of mortality diminishes the urgency and significance of life.

Unity through Eternity: Interconnectedness in an Immortal World

Exploring how an eternal perspective might foster a greater sense of unity and shared purpose among humanity and the planet.

The Aesthetic of the Infinite: Beauty and Creation beyond Time

Reflecting on how endless existence influences creativity, art, and our appreciation of beauty.

Eternity and the Unknown: Embracing Mystery in the Face of Infinity

Concluding with a discussion on the necessity of preserving wonder and curiosity even when confronted with the vastness of endless time.

Introduction

The Quest for Immortality: Science, Ethics, and the Human Psyche

Since the dawn of civilization, humanity has been captivated by the idea of living forever. From ancient myths of the "elixir of life" to the promise of consciousness-uploading through artificial intelligence, the dream of living forever is a thread that runs through our history. But why are we so drawn to it? Perhaps it's the fear of the unknown that comes with death, or maybe it's our innate desire to transcend our limitations. Regardless of the reason, one thing is clear: the quest for living forever reflects both our deepest anxieties and our highest aspirations.

This book is a journey into that quest — a journey that spans ancient wisdom, modern science, and the human psyche itself. While living forever once belonged to the realm of myth and religion, today it is being pursued in the labs of genetic engineers, the minds of AI developers, and the hearts of those who refuse to accept the limits of human life. The pursuit is no longer just about spiritual transcendence; it's also about technological triumph. But at what cost? And to what end?

In this introduction, we will explore three critical dimensions of living forever:

The Science of Immortality:

How advancements in biotechnology, AI, and regenerative medicine are redefining what it means to "age" and "live."

The Ethical Dilemmas of Immortality:

Who gets to live forever, and what are the social, environmental, and thought-provoking consequences of this pursuit?

The Human Psyche and Immortality:

How the idea of eternal life affects our mental well-being, sense of purpose, and perception of what it means to be human.

The Science of Immortality

Breaking the Biological Clock:

Modern science has made extraordinary progress in unraveling the mechanisms of aging. No longer seen as an unavoidable fate, aging is now viewed as a "biological program" that can potentially be reprogrammed, paused, or even reversed. Technologies once considered science fiction are now within reach, and their impact could be transformative.

Advances in Biotechnology:

The science-focused pursuit of living forever focuses on understanding and combating the cellular and molecular processes that drive aging. Three key areas are at the forefront:

Telomere Therapy:

Telomeres, the protective caps on the ends of our chromosomes, shorten as we age. New therapies aim to maintain or restore telomere length, potentially reversing cellular aging.

Senescence Reversal:

Over time, "zombie cells" (senescent cells) accumulate in our bodies, contributing to aging and disease. Anti-senescence drugs (senolytics) are being developed to eliminate these cells, promoting tissue rejuvenation.

Genetic Engineering:

With tools like CRISPR, scientists can edit DNA to correct age-related mutations or enhance human longevity. Genetic modifications could one day enable humans to live significantly longer lives.

Artificial Intelligence and Digital Immortality

If preserving the body proves too difficult, what if we preserved the mind instead? This is the radical idea behind digital living forever. Through AI and machine learning, researchers aim to capture, replicate, and even "upload" human consciousness.

Mind Uploading:

Theoretically, if we could map and simulate every neural connection in the brain, we might be able to upload a person's consciousness into a digital format — a form of "eternal life" in the digital realm.

AI Companions:

Digital avatars, trained on a person's data, memories, and personality traits, could continue to "exist" even after the person has passed. This raises questions about what it means to be "alive" and "human."

Organ Regeneration and Cloning

Why seek living forever through consciousness uploading when we could simply replace failing body parts? Advances in organ regeneration are bringing this idea closer to reality.

3D Bioprinting:

The ability to "print" human organs using a combination of living cells and biomaterials could one day eliminate the need for organ donors.

Stem Cell Therapy:

Regenerative medicine uses stem cells to repair or replace damaged tissues. This could restore health and vitality to aging organs.

These science-focused pursuits seem promising, but they also raise profound ethical and existential questions.

The Ethical Dilemmas of Immortality

What happens if living forever is achieved — but only for some? The possibility of eternal life introduces ethical challenges that go far beyond the individual. How will society change if only the wealthiest can afford to live forever? What impact would a population that never dies have on our planet's resources? And what happens when we "play God" by altering the natural cycle of life and death?

Who Gets to Live Forever?

Not everyone will have equal access to life-extension technologies, and this raises difficult moral questions.

Economic Disparities:

If only the wealthy can afford to live longer, living forever could create new forms of social inequality.

Global Resource Allocation:

A population that lives indefinitely could put immense pressure on food, water, and energy supplies, raising questions about environmental sustainability.

Playing God

Tampering with the natural cycle of life and death forces us to confront existential questions about the purpose and meaning of life.

Natural Order:

Critics argue that death is part of nature's design, and altering it could disrupt the delicate balance of ecosystems and human experience.

AI Ethics:

If AI achieves sentience, should it be granted the same rights as a living being? And if we create “immortal” AI, are we responsible for its well-being?

The Moral Weight of Overpopulation

An immortal human population could pose significant challenges to the planet’s ecosystems and the balance of life on Earth.

Impact on Biodiversity:

Longer human lifespans could lead to habitat destruction and environmental collapse.

Global Equity:

If lifespans are extended for some but not for others, humanity may face growing inequality on a global scale.

The Human Psyche and Immortality

At its core, the quest for living forever is not just about technology — it’s about our relationship with death, meaning, and purpose. Our fear of death drives much of human culture, from art and philosophy to religion and legacy-building. How will the human mind adapt if death is no longer inevitable?

Fear of Death and the Immortality Drive:

Humans are hardwired to fear death, and this fear shapes much of our behaviour.

Terror Management Theory:

This psychological theory proposes that much of human culture — from religion to art — is a way of managing our fear of death.

Legacy and Meaning:

Our desire for legacy — to be remembered after we die — may be the original form of living forever-seeking behaviour.

Psychological Effects of Living Forever

While eternal life sounds appealing, it raises significant psychological challenges.

Loss of Purpose:

Mortality gives life a sense of urgency. Without death, will people lose their sense of direction and purpose?

Boredom and Stagnation:

If life has no end, might people eventually tire of existence? Philosophers like Nietzsche have warned of the "eternal return" — the crushing weight of eternal sameness.

The Influence of AI on the Human Mind

As we become more dependent on AI, it shapes not just our technology but also our minds.

Dependence on Machines:

The more we rely on AI to think, predict, and act on our behalf, the more we may lose touch with our own autonomy and sense of self.

Shifting Definitions of Consciousness:

As AI grows more "human-like," we are forced to confront the question: What is consciousness, and how do we define it?

Bridging Ancient Wisdom and Modern Science

Amid all the technological advancements, it's worth remembering that the concept of living forever isn't new. Ancient spiritual traditions have long explored the idea of transcending death — not by "living forever" but by discovering an immortal essence within us.

Eastern Spiritual Traditions:

Philosophies like Vedanta and Taoism emphasize the timeless nature of the soul. Practices like yoga and meditation aim to connect with this eternal essence.

Balance of Science and Spirit:

By merging ancient wisdom with modern science, we may be able to approach the living forever question more holistically — not just as a quest to "defeat death," but as a path to understand life.

The pursuit of living forever is a reflection of humanity's deepest desires and fears. In the chapters ahead, we will dive deeper into this journey, exploring not just the science but also the right and wrong, psychology, and philosophy of what it means to live forever. As you read, I invite you to ask yourself: Is living forever a goal worth pursuing? And if it is, at what cost.

A New Age of Life Extension: Technology Meets Spirituality

Humanity's timeless aspiration to transcend mortality is entering an unprecedented era, where the promise of ground-breaking technologies converges with the wisdom of ancient spiritual traditions. Modern science offers tools to extend physical life—through genetic engineering, artificial intelligence, and regenerative medicine. Meanwhile, practices like yoga, meditation, and transcendental philosophies provide pathways to inner immortality—anchored in the soul, consciousness, and universal connection.

This exploration delves into the dual pathways of life extension, examining how they intersect, diverge, and collectively redefine the boundaries of life itself.

The Technological Frontier of Life Extension

Pioneering Innovations in Biological Longevity:

Science is transforming aging from an inevitable decline into a solvable challenge:

Epigenetic Reprogramming:

Reversing cellular aging by resetting the biological clock in cells to rejuvenate tissues.

Synthetic Biology:

Engineering artificial biological systems capable of repairing or replacing failing organs.

Nanomedicine:

Deploying nanorobots to repair cells at the molecular level, enhancing organ function and longevity.

AI and Digital Immortality:

Technology introduces radical paradigms for transcending the physical body:

Virtual Consciousness:

Uploading human cognition into digital frameworks for eternal digital existence.

AI-Enhanced Cognition:

Augmenting memory, intellect, and experiences through artificial intelligence.

Human-Robotics Integration:

Fusing human consciousness with cybernetic systems, creating new forms of life.

Challenges of Technological Immortality

Even as it inspires, the technological path raises profound challenges:

Economic Inequities:

Will life extension technologies be accessible to all or reserved for the wealthy?

Dependence on Machines:

How will an over-reliance on technology reshape identity, agency, and what it means to be human?

The Spiritual Approach to Immortality

Ancient Practices for Eternal Life:

Spiritual traditions illuminate a timeless path to inner transcendence:

Yoga and Meditation:

Cultivating union with a universal consciousness that transcends the ego and physical form.

Philosophies of the Soul:

Teachings in Vedanta and Taoism reveal the eternal self as the true source of immortality.

Sacred Rituals:

Rituals that reframe life and death as part of an infinite, cyclical journey.

The Psychological Resilience of Spirituality

Spiritual approaches offer profound tools to confront mortality:

Acceptance of Death:

Embracing death as a natural cycle allows for deeper peace and purpose.

Overcoming Fear:

Inner practices empower individuals to transcend the fear of the unknown, fostering resilience.

Harmonizing Material and Spiritual Goals:

Spirituality reframes the quest for immortality as a journey of balance:

Harmony between Inner and Outer Worlds:

Aligning spiritual growth with technological progress for a holistic perspective on life extension.

Mortality as a Teacher:

Recognizing death as an essential part of life that grants meaning and urgency to existence.

The Intersection: When Technology Meets Spirituality

Bridging the Divide:

The convergence of science and spirituality opens new horizons:

AI-Assisted Mindfulness:

Harnessing AI to deepen meditation and enhance emotional well-being.

Fusion of Wisdoms:

Merging cutting-edge discoveries with timeless philosophies to foster a holistic approach to living forever.

Navigating Ethical and Existential Challenges:

Both paths prompt profound questions about the essence of humanity:

Defining Consciousness:

Can uploading a mind preserve the essence of a soul?

Preserving Humanity:

How do we ensure that progress uplifts, rather than diminishes, the human spirit?

A Unified Perspective:

The future may lie in integrating technology and spirituality:

Tech-Augmented Spiritual Practices:

Using immersive technologies to enhance spiritual experiences.

Philosophy-Driven Science:

Infusing scientific advancements with ethical and spiritual principles to ensure progress benefits humanity as a whole.

The Psyche of the Eternal Being

The Psychological Cost of Immortality:

A life without death may carry unforeseen burdens:

Existential Boredom:

Without mortality, the urgency and purpose of life could fade.

Emotional Isolation:

Outliving loved ones and historical context may lead to profound loneliness.

Transforming Mortality into Meaning

Immortality may be less about living forever and more about changing how we live:

Creating Legacies:

Leaving meaningful impacts—whether through technology or spiritual enlightenment—becomes central to human existence.

Valuing the Present:

Both paths remind us to treasure the fleeting beauty of the present moment.

A New Paradigm for Life Extension

The choice between technology and spirituality in the quest for immortality is not binary. Together, they offer a nuanced and transformative vision of what it means to transcend human limitations. Technology provides the tools to extend life, while spirituality offers the wisdom to enrich it.

As we embark on this extraordinary journey, the ultimate question remains: Can we create a future that not only uplifts our bodies but also nurtures our souls? By integrating the best of science and spirituality, humanity has the opportunity to redefine the essence of life itself—boundless, meaningful, and eternal.

Chapter 1

The Timeless Human Desire for Immortality

The desire for living forever is as old as humanity itself. From ancient spiritual texts to modern science fiction, people have long sought ways to transcend death. This chapter explores two main pathways to living forever: the technological route, which focuses on conquering biological and cognitive limitations, and the spiritual path, which seeks to understand and transcend the self. Despite their differences, these paths may not be as opposed as they seem.

The Technological Path to Immortality

Modern technology has transformed living forever from myth to potential reality. With advances in biology, artificial intelligence, and data science, humanity is beginning to imagine a world where aging and death are no longer inevitable.

The Science of Longevity:

Scientific advancements have redefined aging as a treatable, and possibly reversible, condition. This section delves into the key pillars of longevity research:

Regenerative Medicine:

Regenerative medicine focuses on repairing and replacing damaged tissues and organs, often using the body's own cells.

Stem Cell Therapies:

Stem cells have the ability to regenerate damaged tissues, making them critical to organ repair and regeneration.

Tissue Engineering:

By growing organs in a lab using 3D bioprinting, scientists may one day create organs on demand, eliminating the need for transplants.

Organ Replacement:

Advances in xenotransplantation (using animal organs) and lab-grown organs could end the global organ shortage.

Gene Therapy and Genetic Engineering:

CRISPR and Gene Editing: With CRISPR, scientists can now target and modify specific genes responsible for aging. This opens possibilities for correcting genetic defects and slowing down cellular aging.

Telomere Extension:

Telomeres, the "caps" at the end of chromosomes, shorten with age. By lengthening them, it may be possible to extend cell life and delay aging.

Senescence Inhibition:

Senolytics: Certain drugs can target "zombie cells" (senescent cells) that accumulate in tissues and contribute to aging. Eliminating these cells can promote tissue regeneration and slow down degenerative diseases.

The Digital Revolution in Immortality:

While biological living forever focuses on the body, digital living forever aims to preserve consciousness, memory, and personal identity. By transforming the mind into data, people could exist forever in digital form.

Mind Uploading:

This speculative idea involves scanning the human brain and uploading its neural patterns to a digital medium. In theory, the uploaded mind could continue to exist even if the original body dies.

Companies like Nectome are working on "preservation" methods to store the human brain for future scanning and digitization.

AI Avatars and Virtual Afterlives:

Using AI, people can create "digital twins" — avatars that mimic the personality, thoughts, and behaviours of a real person. These avatars could continue to "live" after the person's death, simulating conversations and relationships.

Some companies, like Replika, already offer AI companions, hinting at how future AI avatars may preserve an individual's essence.

Cyborg Integration:

Neural implants like Elon Musk's Neuralink aim to enhance human cognition by connecting the brain directly to computers.

As human cognition merges with artificial intelligence, the boundary between human and machine may blur, creating a "cyborg" existence that can evolve over time.

The Ethical Challenges of Technology:

Technological living forever presents profound ethical questions that affect individuals, society, and the planet.

Access Inequality:

Will only the wealthy be able to afford life-extending technologies, further widening the gap between rich and poor?

Will governments regulate access, or will this technology become a privilege for elites?

Identity and Consciousness:

If your consciousness is uploaded into a computer, is it still you? Or is it merely a digital copy?

Philosophers and neuroscientists debate whether continuity of self can survive digital replication.

Environmental Impact:

Immortal humans could exacerbate overpopulation, leading to higher resource consumption.

Could endless life hinder humanity's ability to prioritize environmental stewardship?

The Spiritual Pursuit of Immortality

While technology seeks to "defeat" death, spirituality seeks to understand and accept it. Many spiritual traditions view death not as an end, but as a transition. Immortality, according to these traditions, does not require living forever in the body—it is about realizing the eternal nature of the soul.

Ancient Wisdom and Eternal Life:

Transcendental Practices:

Spiritual disciplines like yoga, meditation, and breathwork aim to achieve a state of consciousness beyond the limitations of the body.

Advanced practitioners of yoga claim to experience "timeless" states of being where past, present, and future merge into one eternal moment.

The Soul's Journey:

Vedanta, a school of Hindu philosophy, teaches that the "Atman" (soul) is eternal and never truly dies. This aligns with similar teachings in Taoism and Buddhism.

Instead of fearing death, followers are encouraged to recognize their soul's timeless nature.

Rituals and Symbolism:

Rituals around life, death, and rebirth are common in nearly every spiritual tradition, reinforcing the idea that living forever can be achieved through spiritual connection, legacy, and the afterlife.

Spiritual Resilience in the Face of Mortality:

Acceptance of Death:

Unlike technological living forever, spiritual traditions view death as a natural and necessary process.

By accepting mortality, people achieve peace of mind and freedom from existential anxiety.

The Power of Presence:

Living fully in the present moment is seen as a way to "transcend" death. Meditation teaches people to release their fear of the future and fully embrace each moment.

Legacy through Connection:

Spiritual living forever is also achieved by leaving behind a lasting legacy — not through living forever, but through the impact one has on others.

Contributions to art, wisdom, and love ensure that a person's influence lives on in the lives of future generations.

Limitations of the Spiritual Approach:

Non-Universal Appeal:

Not everyone subscribes to spiritual worldviews, which are often deeply personal.

For people who reject religious or spiritual concepts, the idea of "soul living forever" may feel unconvincing.

Abstract vs. Tangible:

Unlike technological living forever, which offers physical evidence (like lab-grown organs or mind-uploading theories), spiritual living forever depends on belief and faith.

Crossroads: Convergence or Divergence?

Where Science and Spirituality Meet:

Despite their differences, science and spirituality often seek similar goals:

Understanding Consciousness:

Both paths seek to understand the nature of self-awareness and consciousness.

Enhancing Well-being:

Science aims to extend lifespan; spirituality focuses on achieving quality of life through peace and fulfilment.

Seeking Legacy:

Both seek to "live on" beyond death—whether through digital avatars, science-focused contributions, or spiritual influence.

Techno-Spiritual Fusion:

Modern technology is blending with spiritual practice in unprecedented ways:

Mindfulness Apps:

Apps like Headspace guide users in meditation, a practice rooted in ancient spiritual teachings.

Immersive Experiences:

Virtual reality simulations offer experiences of transcendence and "mystical" states, similar to deep meditative practices.

Philosophy-Inspired Design:

Ethical AI and life-extension technologies are beginning to draw inspiration from moral philosophy and ancient wisdom.

Potential Conflicts:

Despite their overlap, science and spirituality diverge in key ways:

The Value of Mortality:

Spirituality often views death as essential for life's meaning, while technology seeks to "defeat" it.

Dependence on Technology:

If humanity becomes overly reliant on machines for well-being, spiritual growth and resilience may decline.

Psychological Implications of Extended Life

The prospect of living forever, or for significantly extended periods of time, brings with it profound psychological questions and challenges. Beyond the science-focused and ethical debates, the psychological impact of living forever — whether achieved through technology or spirituality — is something that must be carefully considered. What happens to human purpose, identity, and mental well-being when death is no longer an inevitable part of life? The idea of living forever not only affects the body but also reshapes the very foundation of the human psyche.

Reimagining Life's Purpose:

An extended lifespan forces a dramatic rethinking of what it means to live a fulfilling life. If the human experience were to span centuries, traditional milestones like marriage, career progression, and retirement would become antiquated concepts. People may need to redefine what it means to grow, evolve, and find meaning in a life without a natural end.

Shifting Milestones:

Relationships:

What would relationships look like in a world where people live far beyond their current life expectancy? Would romantic bonds, friendships, and family structures evolve into long-term, ever-changing dynamics? How would the expectations of generations shift when life itself is prolonged indefinitely?

Careers:

Career paths, too, would undergo radical transformations. People may embark on multiple careers across their extended lives, continually reinventing themselves and their aspirations.

Personal Growth:

Would the concept of personal growth become endless, with no natural time limits to goals, achievements, or self-improvement? Would living forever lead to perpetual self-development or an eventual sense of stagnation?

Existential Crises:

The Risk of Stagnation:

With infinite time at one's disposal, the constant pursuit of goals and passions may lose their urgency. Immortality could intensify feelings of ennui or dissatisfaction, as the individual might confront a lack of purpose or drive.

A Crisis of Purpose:

The human experience is often shaped by the inevitability of death, which gives our actions meaning. Without this looming endpoint, people may struggle to find purpose. How do we keep our sense of urgency, ambition, and fulfilment alive when there is no "end" to our journey? Would the meaning of life become less impactful if we are able to stretch it infinitely?

Mental Health in the Immortal Age:

While technology or spiritual paths to living forever may seem appealing, they come with their own set of psychological burdens. Extended life could lead to unforeseen mental health challenges that require careful attention.

Coping with Loss:

The Emotional Toll of Outliving Loved Ones: Immortality would necessitate coming to terms with the death of friends, family, and entire generations. While the immortal individual remains, their loved ones — and their connections — may not. The loss of relationships, both intimate and generational, could leave deep emotional scars and foster feelings of loneliness.

Witnessing the Passage of Time:

Over centuries, the immortal individual may experience deep sadness or frustration as the world around them changes, sometimes beyond recognition. The perpetual loss of loved ones could lead to a profound sense of grief and isolation.

Preserving Identity:

Constant Change:

Prolonged existence would inevitably lead to profound changes in the self. The individual may go through numerous reinventions and transformations over the course of centuries. How does one maintain a cohesive sense of identity when everything — including physical appearance, mental faculties, and interests — is in flux?

The Challenge of Consistency:

Without the natural rhythms of life and death, people may find it difficult to maintain a steady sense of self. Identity may become fragmented or diluted, leading to a loss of continuity in personal history and experiences.

The Role of AI in the Psyche:

As technology continues to advance, AI could play an increasingly significant role in shaping the mental and emotional landscape of living forever. From augmenting human cognition to potentially offering emotional support, AI introduces both exciting possibilities and intriguing challenges for the human mind.

Augmented Consciousness:

Memory Enhancement:

AI tools could expand cognitive abilities, offering the potential to store and recall memories with perfect clarity. The boundaries between human and machine may blur, with AI providing not just enhanced memory but also the ability to augment reasoning and creativity. However, this reliance on AI could raise questions about the nature of human thought and whether these "enhanced" minds would retain their authentic self.

Cognitive Transformation:

With AI tools directly interfacing with the human brain, individuals may gain access to skills and knowledge previously out of reach. This could accelerate learning, creativity, and problem-solving, leading to rapid intellectual development.

However, the potential erosion of human autonomy — as AI plays an increasingly dominant role — could lead to psychological concerns about free will and agency.

Emotional AI:

Companionship in the Digital Age: AI-powered avatars or companions may offer emotional support, providing individuals with a constant, understanding presence. These digital beings could be programmed to simulate empathy, offering comfort and companionship to counter the emotional isolation that might come with extended life.

Authenticity and Connection:

While these AI companions could provide solace, they may also present emotional complications. Can a digital avatar truly replace the depth of human connection? Will individuals grow emotionally dependent on AI, losing the capacity for authentic relationships with real people?

A Defining Challenge of Our Time

The pursuit of living forever, whether through technological or spiritual means, is a defining challenge of our time. Technology presents opportunities to conquer disease, aging, and death, offering the possibility of an indefinite lifespan. But with these opportunities come profound ethical dilemmas and psychological implications. The promise of extended life brings not only the hope of defeating death but also the responsibility to consider its effects on the human psyche.

Spiritual paths, grounded in ancient wisdom, provide timeless tools for navigating the human condition. They offer a framework for understanding life and death that transcends physical existence. Yet, for many, the spiritual path may not hold the same appeal as science-focused advancements with tangible, measurable outcomes.

Ultimately, technology and spirituality need not be in opposition. In fact, they can complement each other, offering a holistic approach to living forever. A balanced integration of both could enrich not only our lifespans but also the depth and quality of our lives.

By embracing both the advancements of technology and the wisdom of spiritual teachings, humanity can create a future that goes beyond the mere extension of life — a future that nurtures the soul, mind, and body, as they transcend the boundaries of biology and consciousness.

The Roots of Immortality: Ancient Philosophies and Spiritual Wisdom

The quest for living forever has been a central theme in human civilization throughout history, woven into the fabric of our myths, philosophies, and spiritual practices. This longing for eternal life is not merely rooted in a fear of death but is also a profound desire to transcend the limits of the physical body, to connect with a greater universal consciousness, and to uncover the deeper meaning of existence. Ancient cultures have expressed the pursuit of living forever in diverse ways, reflecting varied understandings of life, death, and the afterlife. This section explores the ancient roots of the human desire for living forever, investigating how spiritual traditions and thought-provoking schools have conceptualized and sought to achieve eternal existence. These timeless teachings continue to shape modern perspectives on living forever, offering insights into the psychological and ethical dimensions of our aspirations for eternal life.

Immortality in Myth and Legend

The Quest for Eternal Life:

Mesopotamian Epics:

The Epic of Gilgamesh, one of the earliest literary works in human history, chronicles the hero's search for living forever. Gilgamesh's quest, driven by the death of his friend Enkidu, reflects humanity's struggle to reconcile with the inevitability of death and the deep yearning for eternal meaning. The story reveals the tension between mortal limitations and the desire to transcend them, emphasizing that living forever is a divine gift, not a human right. Gilgamesh's journey, culminating in the realization that living forever lies not in escaping death but in living a meaningful life, provides an ancient thought-provoking reflection on the nature of death and legacy.

Greek Myths:

In Greek mythology, tales like that of Tithonus, who was granted eternal life without eternal youth, serve as cautionary stories. His immortal existence is marked by endless aging and suffering, symbolizing the unintended consequences of living forever. The myth of Tithonus underscores the Greek belief that living forever, when granted without wisdom or balance, leads to tragic outcomes. Similarly, the story of Hercules, who achieved living forever after completing his twelve labours, reflects the intertwining of heroic virtue and eternal life.

Eastern Legends:

In Taoist and Chinese mythology, living forever is often intertwined with alchemy, spiritual enlightenment, and the search for elixirs of life. Legendary figures like Xu Fu, who sought the elixir of living forever for the emperor, and immortal sages, who achieved transcendence, highlight the Taoist vision of living forever as a spiritual attunement. Unlike the Greek myths, these Eastern legends often focus on inner transformation and harmony with the universe as the key to achieving eternal life.

Symbolism in Immortality Myths

The Tree of Life:

This symbol is universally found across cultures, representing the interconnection of all forms of life and the cyclical nature of existence. The Tree of Life often symbolizes regeneration, resurrection, and the eternal continuity of life. In the Epic of Gilgamesh, for instance, the tree of living forever serves as a symbol of life's renewal. Similarly, in the Kabbalistic Tree of Life, the structure of creation itself is mapped out in a way that shows the possibility of achieving enlightenment and spiritual living forever.

Phoenix and Rebirth:

The Phoenix, a bird that burns itself to death and is reborn from its ashes, is a powerful metaphor for cyclical living forever. This symbolizes not just physical rebirth but the thought-provoking idea of transformation, where living forever is achieved not by static continuation, but through perpetual renewal. This concept of cyclic regeneration is echoed in various spiritual and mystical traditions, emphasizing the theme of spiritual resurrection over the simplistic idea of an unending physical existence.

Philosophical Foundations of Immortality

Immortality in Eastern Philosophies:

Vedantic Teachings:

In ancient Indian philosophy, particularly within the Vedanta, living forever is conceived as the eternal nature of the soul (Atman). The soul is indestructible and distinct from the transient physical body. The pursuit of living forever, according to Vedanta, is through spiritual realization of the unity of the Atman with Brahman, the ultimate reality. The belief in reincarnation highlights the continuity of the soul's existence across multiple lifetimes. The true path to living forever is the realization of oneness with the universe, freeing oneself from the cycle of birth and death (Samsara).

Taoism:

Taoist philosophies emphasize living forever not as a physical state, but as spiritual enlightenment. Immortality, in Taoism, is seen as the ability to harmonize with the flow of the universe, known as the Tao. The quest for living forever in Taoism involves practices such as meditation, breath control, Qi Gong, and alchemical rituals designed to cultivate vitality and achieve spiritual transcendence. Taoist alchemy sought to refine the inner energies of the body to attain spiritual living forever, viewed as a higher state of consciousness rather than physical endurance.

Buddhism:

Buddhism challenges the conventional notion of living forever by presenting the idea of impermanence (Anicca). The Buddhist perspective holds that attachment to a permanent self is the root of suffering, and living forever is not the continuation of the individual self, but liberation from the endless cycle of Samsara (the cycle of birth, death, and rebirth). Immortality, therefore, is the achievement of Nirvana, a state of enlightenment where the soul is free from suffering and the illusion of self. Thus, in Buddhism, living forever is not about physical survival but transcendence beyond existence itself.

Immortality in Western Thought:

Platonic Ideals:

Plato, in his thought-provoking works such as the Phaedo, proposed that the soul is eternal, pre-existing the body and continuing after physical death. For Plato, intellectual and moral excellence were pathways to living forever. He argued that true knowledge, virtue, and thought-provoking wisdom lead to the soul's living forever, where the soul is freed from the constraints of the body and attains a higher form of existence.

Stoicism:

The Stoic philosophers, like Epictetus and Marcus Aurelius, emphasized the importance of living in harmony with nature, reason, and virtue. They proposed that living forever lies in the legacy one leaves through virtuous actions, ideas, and service to humanity. The Stoics did not believe in physical living forever but rather in an immortal cosmic order and an eternal connection to the logos (the rational principle governing the universe). To the Stoics, living forever was achieved through aligning oneself with this divine reason, living a life of integrity and wisdom.

Christian Theology:

Christianity teaches that eternal life is achieved through divine grace and the promise of resurrection. According to Christian doctrine, salvation and living forever come through faith in Christ and adherence to spiritual and moral principles. The Christian concept of living forever is not based on the perpetual continuation of earthly life but on the belief in the resurrection of the body and the soul's eternal life with God in the afterlife. This vision of living forever emphasizes faith, redemption, and divine grace.

Practices Rooted in Spiritual Wisdom:

Inner Practices for Transcendence:

Yoga and Meditation:

In ancient Indian traditions, practices like Yoga and Meditation were specifically developed to transcend the limitations of the body and the mind. These practices, aiming to quiet the mind and align with the Atman, provide a direct experience of spiritual living forever.

Hatha Yoga, Kundalini Yoga, and Jnana Yoga offer paths to transcend the physical body's constraints, allowing one to experience the eternal self. Meditation practices like Vipassana and Zazen also focus on inner stillness and awakening to a state of spiritual awareness that connects the practitioner to the timeless nature of the soul.

Prayer and Chanting:

Prayer, recitation of mantras, and chanting have been central to many religious and spiritual traditions across the world. These practices are believed to facilitate a direct connection with the divine, cultivate mindfulness, and reinforce the concept of eternal truth. In Hinduism,

Japa (the repetition of a mantra) is a tool to focus the mind on the divine, while in Christianity, the practice of contemplative prayer connects individuals to the eternal presence of God.

Alchemical and Mystical Traditions:

Alchemy:

In both Eastern and Western traditions, alchemy is closely tied to the pursuit of living forever. Alchemists sought the Philosopher's Stone, a mythical substance believed to grant eternal life by transforming base metals into gold or creating an elixir of life. In Taoist alchemy, practices were centered on refining internal energies (Qi) to cultivate living forever. Western alchemical traditions, particularly during the Renaissance, viewed spiritual enlightenment and living forever as the transmutation of the soul's impurities into divine light.

Mysticism:

Mystics across cultures, such as Sufi, Kabbalistic, and Christian mystics, describe the union of the individual soul with the divine as a state of eternal existence. Rumi, the famous Sufi poet, wrote extensively about the soul's journey towards union with the divine, which can be seen as an experience of spiritual living forever. Similarly, Kabbalah teaches that through mystical practices, the soul can reunite with God and attain an immortal state beyond the limitations of physical existence.

Rituals and Ceremonies:

Ancestral Worship:

Many cultures, particularly in African, Asian, and indigenous traditions, view living forever as a spiritual continuity through ancestral reverence. By honoring ancestors through rituals, offerings, and prayers, these cultures maintain an ongoing connection with the spiritual world, ensuring the continuation of life through memory and reverence.

Death as Transformation:

In many traditions, death is not seen as an end but as a transformation of the soul. The Egyptian and Greek rites of passage, for example, saw death as the transition to another realm where the soul could continue its journey. Similarly, in Taoism and Buddhism, death represents a passing through a portal of transcendence toward spiritual living forever.

Ethical and Psychological Dimensions of Ancient Wisdom

The Role of Mortality in Meaning:

Stoic Reflections:

The Stoic philosophers believed that mortality is central to living a virtuous life. The awareness of death is a catalyst for personal growth, urging individuals to live meaningfully and pursue virtue, knowing that every moment is finite.

Buddhist Impermanence:

Buddhism teaches that all things are impermanent, and by accepting the transient nature of life, we can reduce attachment and suffering. In this context, living forever is not about an endless existence but about transcending attachment and entering a state of enlightened peace.

Ethical Implications of Pursuing Immortality:

Balance with Nature:

Taoist teachings emphasize the importance of living in harmony with nature, warning against disrupting the natural order in the pursuit of longevity. Immortality achieved through artificial means is seen as unnatural and destabilizing.

Moral Responsibility:

Immortality is considered meaningful only when aligned with ethical living, moral responsibility, and service to others. Many ancient philosophies caution against the pursuit of living forever for selfish reasons, emphasizing the importance of living for the benefit of others.

Psychological Insights from Spiritual Teachings:

Coping with Mortality:

Ancient spiritual practices such as mindfulness, contemplation, and meditation provide individuals with the tools to face mortality with resilience. These practices help cultivate an inner peace that transcends the fear of death.

Expanding Consciousness:

Many spiritual traditions emphasize the importance of transcending the ego, which is often seen as the barrier between the individual self and the infinite consciousness. Through practices that expand awareness and connect individuals to the eternal, a sense of living forever is achieved through union with the divine or universal consciousness.

Relevance to Modern Pursuits of Immortality

Continuities with Modern Science:

The Philosophical Underpinnings of Biotech:

Modern biotech research into life extension, including efforts to slow aging and rejuvenate cells, echoes ancient desires for living forever. Philosophically, these science-focused pursuits seek to preserve the essence of life, paralleling ancient efforts to prolong existence.

Integration with AI:

Artificial intelligence (AI) has begun to integrate spiritual practices, such as meditation and mindfulness, into its platforms, offering digital tools that support the pursuit of mental and spiritual longevity. Some contemporary technologies, such as virtual living forever, reflect the ancient desire for a form of existence beyond the physical body.

Lessons for the Present:

Holistic Approaches:

Modern technologies, when coupled with ethical and spiritual practices, offer a more holistic path to living forever. By balancing technological advances with spiritual wisdom, we can address the multi-faceted nature of human existence.

Focus on the Present:

Ancient wisdom teaches that the most important aspect of living forever is how we live today. Living fully, with mindfulness and purpose, is central to a fulfilling life, even as we seek to extend it.

The quest for living forever, as explored through ancient philosophies and spiritual wisdom, reveals that the pursuit of eternal life is not merely about prolonging physical existence. It is about understanding the deeper nature of life, aligning with universal truths, and transcending the limits of the individual self. These teachings offer profound insights into the ethical, psychological, and spiritual dimensions of living forever, which remain highly relevant as we explore modern avenues for extending life. Ultimately, the journey towards living forever is about enriching life, fostering connection, and finding peace within the eternal rhythms of existence.

Immortality in Eastern Traditions: Yoga, Vedanta, and Beyond

Eastern spiritual traditions provide a profound and multi-faceted understanding of living forever that transcends the mere extension of physical life. These traditions focus on the concept of transcending the mortal self, achieving unity with the eternal, and liberating individuals from the cycle of birth, death, and rebirth. The spiritual teachings in Yoga, Vedanta, Taoism, Buddhism, and other Eastern philosophies present living forever not as a physical or biological phenomenon, but as a realization of the eternal nature of consciousness and the interconnectedness of existence. This section explores the diverse views on living forever within Eastern traditions and examines how they remain relevant in contemporary life, particularly in the context of modern wellness, longevity, and the search for deeper meaning.

The Core Philosophy of Immortality in Eastern Thought

Understanding the Eternal Self:

Atman and Brahman in Vedanta:

In Vedanta, a foundational thought-provoking school in Hinduism, living forever is understood as the realization of the unity between the individual soul (Atman) and the universal consciousness (Brahman). The Atman is eternal, indestructible, and beyond birth and death. According to Vedantic philosophy, the cycle of birth, death, and rebirth (Samsara) is an illusion (Maya) created by ignorance (Avidya). True living forever is realized through spiritual awakening, which involves understanding the inherent oneness of the Atman with Brahman. This realization leads to liberation (Moksha), where the individual transcends the cycle of rebirth and merges with the divine consciousness, experiencing living forever through unity with the eternal.

The Nature of Samsara:

In Vedanta and many other Eastern philosophies, Samsara is seen as the cyclical process of birth, death, and reincarnation. This cycle is driven by Karma, the law of cause and effect, and is fueled by the ignorance of the true nature of the self. Mortality, in this sense, is not a fundamental aspect of human nature but a condition resulting from ignorance. By gaining knowledge of one's true nature and realizing the illusory nature of material existence, one can escape Samsara and achieve Moksha, which is the essence of spiritual living forever.

Taoist Eternal Flow:

Taoism presents living forever as merging with the Tao—the eternal, unchanging, and all-encompassing source of all existence. In Taoist philosophy, living forever is not about physical longevity but about aligning oneself with the Tao's natural flow, transcending the limitations of the body, and merging with the cosmic order.

Taoist living forever is about living harmoniously with nature and the Tao, understanding that life and death are part of a natural cycle, and embracing the flow of energy that pervades the universe.

The Role of Impermanence:

Eastern traditions emphasize that understanding impermanence is central to achieving living forever:

Buddhist Anicca (Impermanence):

In Buddhism, the concept of Anicca (impermanence) teaches that all phenomena are transient and subject to change. The recognition of impermanence leads to the understanding that attachment to transient things causes suffering (Dukkha). By acknowledging the impermanence of the body and the material world, individuals can cultivate detachment, reduce their attachments to the ego and physical existence, and work towards spiritual liberation (Nirvana). In Buddhism, living forever is not about preserving the body, but rather transcending attachment to the self and attaining freedom from the cycle of rebirth.

Zen Perspectives:

Zen Buddhism takes a unique approach to living forever by focusing on the present moment. Zen practitioners believe that living forever is not about living forever but about being fully immersed in the eternal present. Through Zazen (seated meditation) and mindfulness, Zen practitioners aim to experience a direct realization of the interconnectedness of all things, including life and death. Immortality, in this sense, is the recognition of the timeless nature of consciousness and the awareness of the impermanence of all things.

Yoga: The Path to Eternal Consciousness

The Philosophy of Yoga:

Yoga is a spiritual and thought-provoking system designed to help individuals transcend the limitations of the physical body and mind, ultimately leading to union with the eternal consciousness.

Patanjali's Yoga Sutras:

The Yoga Sutras of Patanjali outlines an eightfold path (Ashtanga Yoga) that provides a systematic approach to spiritual liberation. The path involves ethical disciplines (Yamas and Niyamas), physical postures (Asanas), breath control (Pranayama), sensory withdrawal (Pratyahara), concentration (Dharana), meditation (Dhyana), and ultimately, self-realization (Samadhi). Samadhi is the state of deep, uninterrupted meditation in which the individual consciousness merges with the universal consciousness, leading to liberation and living forever in the form of eternal awareness.

Kundalini Awakening:

Kundalini Yoga focuses on awakening the dormant spiritual energy (Kundalini) at the base of the spine. Through practices like breath control, meditation, and asanas, this energy is believed to rise up the spine, activating higher states of consciousness and leading to a state of self-realization and union with the divine. Kundalini awakening is seen as a process of spiritual living forever, as it connects the individual soul with the universal consciousness and transcends the limitations of the physical body.

Practices Leading to Immortality:

Pranayama (Breath Control):

In Yoga, breath control is a fundamental practice for expanding life force (Prana) and extending life energy. Techniques like Anulom Vilom (alternate nostril breathing) and Kapalbhati (skull shining breath) are designed to purify the body and mind, increase vitality, and promote longevity. Breath control also helps practitioners attain a higher state of consciousness by calming the mind and facilitating meditation.

Asana (Postures):

The physical postures (Asanas) in Yoga prepare the body for higher meditative states and help maintain physical health and flexibility. Asanas open up energy channels in the body, allowing the flow of Prana to nourish the body and mind. Practices like Surya Namaskar (sun salutations) and Padmasana (lotus posture) are especially designed to align the body with the higher energy frequencies required for spiritual awakening.

Dhyana and Samadhi:

Meditation (Dhyana) and the ultimate state of Samadhi are the tools for achieving transcendence in Yoga. Samadhi represents the dissolution of the ego and the merging of individual consciousness with the universal consciousness. This is seen as a form of living forever, where the practitioner realizes their eternal nature and existence beyond the physical body.

Yogic Insights on Modern Longevity:

Mind-Body Harmony:

Yoga promotes the harmony of mind and body, emphasizing both physical health and mental resilience. By engaging in regular Yoga practice, individuals can reduce stress, improve cardiovascular health, and strengthen the immune system, all of which contribute to longevity. The Yogic concept of Sattva (purity) encourages balanced living, which leads to long life and mental clarity.

Relevance to Modern Science:

Modern neuroscience has validated many Yogic practices, especially meditation, for their positive effects on brain function, stress reduction, and overall well-being.

Studies have shown that regular meditation can lower cortisol levels, enhance cognitive function, and promote emotional well-being, all of which contribute to improved longevity and mental clarity.

Vedanta: Liberation and the Eternal Self

Core Teachings of Vedanta:

Vedanta explores the eternal nature of existence and teaches that the ultimate reality is non-dual, and that there is no separation between the individual soul (Atman) and the universal consciousness (Brahman).

Non-Dualism (Advaita):

Advaita Vedanta, the most prominent school of Vedanta, teaches that the apparent differences between the individual self and the universe are illusions.

When a person realizes that their true nature is Brahman, eternal, infinite, and unchanging—they achieve living forever. This realization leads to Moksha, liberation from the cycle of birth and death.

Liberation through Knowledge:

In Vedanta, living forever is achieved not through physical means but through the cultivation of Jnana (knowledge). By gaining true knowledge of the self and recognizing one's unity with Brahman, a person transcends the ego and attains liberation. The ultimate goal is to experience the unchanging, eternal truth that exists beyond the illusion of the material world.

Practical Pathways to Moksha:

Self-Inquiry (Atma Vichara):

One of the key practices in Vedanta is the technique of self-inquiry, particularly as taught by the sage Ramana Maharshi. This practice involves asking oneself "Who am I?" and investigating the nature of the self. By piercing through the layers of ego, thought, and identification with the body, a practitioner realizes their true, eternal nature.

Devotion (Bhakti Yoga):

While Vedanta emphasizes knowledge, Bhakti Yoga offers a path of devotion to the divine. By cultivating love and devotion to God, practitioners surrender their ego and dissolve their individuality, ultimately merging with the divine consciousness and attaining living forever.

Detachment (Vairagya):

Detachment from material possessions, desires, and attachments is essential for spiritual growth. By letting go of the false identification with the body and the material world, one transcends the cycle of birth and death and attains eternal freedom.

Vedanta's Influence on Modern Philosophy:

Vedantic ideas have influenced Western thinkers such as Aldous Huxley, Carl Jung, and Ralph Waldo Emerson. Huxley, in particular, explored Vedanta in his works, discussing the possibility of expanding consciousness and attaining a higher state of awareness. The influence of Vedanta on modern philosophy has helped shape global perspectives on living forever, consciousness, and the nature of existence.

Beyond Yoga and Vedanta: Other Eastern Traditions

Taoist Immortality:

Harmony with the Tao:

Taoism teaches that living forever is achieved by aligning oneself with the Tao, the natural flow of the universe. Immortality in Taoism is not about avoiding death, but about merging with the eternal Tao, recognizing the unity of life and death as part of the natural cycle.

Alchemy and Longevity Practices:

Taoist living forever practices involve internal alchemy, where physical and spiritual energy are cultivated to achieve harmony. Practices like Qi Gong, herbal medicine, and breathing exercises help cultivate internal energy (Qi), which is believed to lead to longevity and spiritual living forever.

Buddhist Perspectives on Liberation:

Nirvana as Immortality:

In Buddhism, living forever is viewed as freedom from the cycle of birth, death, and rebirth (Samsara). Nirvana, the ultimate goal in Buddhism, represents the cessation of suffering and the realization

The Western Scientific Pursuit of Eternal Life

In Western thought, the quest for living forever has evolved from ancient myths and religious dogma to the domain of rigorous science-focused inquiry. Unlike Eastern spiritual practices, which focus on transcendence and liberation from the cycle of existence, the Western science-focused approach often centres on extending biological life, preventing disease, and reversing the aging process. From early alchemical practices to modern breakthroughs in biotechnology and regenerative medicine, the Western pursuit of living forever has undergone profound transformations. This section delves into the historical roots, key science-focused advancements, current technologies, and ethical dilemmas surrounding the pursuit of biological living forever.

Historical Foundations of Scientific Immortality

The Alchemical Quest:

Alchemy as Proto-Science:

In medieval Europe, alchemists were pioneers in early chemical experimentation. Their most famous goal—the creation of the philosopher's stone—was believed to grant eternal life and transmute base metals into gold. Although alchemy was steeped in mystical beliefs, it laid the foundation for modern chemistry, pharmacology, and the science-focused study of aging and longevity.

Paracelsus and Longevity:

Paracelsus, a Swiss physician and alchemist, took a more practical approach by integrating alchemical concepts with medical practices. He advanced the idea that health and longevity could be achieved by harmonizing the body's internal chemistry, influencing early science-focused ideas about life extension.

Enlightenment and Rationalism:

Advances in Anatomy:

The Renaissance and Enlightenment periods saw significant strides in the study of human anatomy. Pioneers like Andreas Vesalius and William Harvey debunked many superstitions surrounding the body and its functions. This approach paved the way for understanding the human body as a biological machine, setting the stage for the study of aging and longevity through science-focused means.

Francis Bacon's Vision:

Philosopher and statesman Francis Bacon, often regarded as the father of the science-focused method, envisioned a future in which science would not only improve the human condition but would ultimately conquer aging and death.

His work inspired the early development of experimental medicine and the eventual pursuit of life extension technologies.

Key Breakthroughs in Longevity Research

The Advent of Modern Medicine:

Vaccines and Disease Control:

The development of vaccines in the 18th and 19th centuries (e.g., smallpox vaccine) dramatically reduced mortality rates, thus contributing to the extension of life expectancy. The ability to control infectious diseases helped lay the groundwork for a longer, healthier life, moving closer to the concept of life extension.

Antibiotics and Public Health:

The discovery of antibiotics, such as penicillin in 1928, revolutionized medical science and drastically reduced deaths from bacterial infections. Coupled with advancements in sanitation and hygiene, these developments resulted in some of the first significant increases in average lifespan.

Understanding Aging: Biology and Genetics:

The Discovery of DNA:

The discovery of the structure of DNA in 1953 by James Watson and Francis Crick unveiled the molecular basis of heredity and genetic inheritance. This landmark breakthrough opened doors to genetic engineering, with the potential to manipulate genes that control aging and age-related diseases.

Telomeres and Cellular Aging:

In the 1970s, researchers discovered telomeres—protective caps at the ends of chromosomes that shorten as cells divide. This process is now recognized as one of the central mechanisms behind aging. Telomeres have since become a major focus in the search for ways to slow down or reverse aging at the cellular level.

Regenerative Medicine:

Stem Cell Therapy:

Stem cell therapy holds significant promise for life extension, as these undifferentiated cells have the potential to regenerate damaged tissues and organs. Advances in stem cell research have already led to promising treatments for degenerative diseases, such as Parkinson's disease, and heart damage caused by aging.

Organ Regeneration and Transplants:

Biotechnological advancements in organ engineering, as well as developments in transplantation, have already extended the lives of many individuals.

These technologies continue to improve, with bioengineered organs potentially offering a future solution to age-related organ failure.

The Current State of the Scientific Quest

Biotechnological Advancements:

CRISPR and Gene Editing:

The advent of CRISPR-Cas9 technology, a revolutionary gene-editing tool, has allowed scientists to make precise alterations to the DNA sequence of living organisms. This has significant implications for aging research, as researchers can now target genes associated with age-related diseases and potentially reverse or delay aging.

Senescence Research:

One of the most exciting areas of research in longevity is senescence—the process by which cells stop dividing and become dysfunctional. Researchers are exploring ways to remove senescent cells from the body or rejuvenate them, which could significantly slow down the aging process.

Artificial Intelligence and Big Data

AI in Longevity Research:

Artificial intelligence is playing an increasingly important role in longevity research. Machine learning algorithms can analyze vast datasets to identify biomarkers of aging, predict age-related diseases, and suggest interventions to slow down or reverse aging. AI is also being used to accelerate drug discovery for anti-aging treatments.

Predictive Healthcare:

Personalized medicine, enabled by big data analytics and AI, is revolutionizing healthcare. Machine learning models can predict which individuals are most likely to develop age-related conditions, enabling early interventions that extend healthspan.

The Rise of Anti-Aging Pharmaceuticals:

Rapamycin and Metformin:

Drugs like Rapamycin (originally used as an immunosuppressant) and Metformin (a diabetes medication) have shown promise in extending lifespan in animal models. Both drugs are now being tested in human clinical trials for their potential to delay aging and improve healthspan.

NAD+ Boosters:

Nicotinamide Adenine Dinucleotide (NAD+) is a molecule involved in cellular energy production and repair. As we age, NAD+ levels decline, contributing to aging and age-related diseases. Researchers are exploring NAD+ boosters to enhance cellular repair mechanisms and extend life.

Emerging Paradigms in Life Extension

Cyborgization: Merging Man and Machine:

Prosthetics and Neural Interfaces:

The integration of advanced prosthetics and neural interfaces is extending the physical and cognitive capabilities of the human body. Brain-machine interfaces (BMIs) are allowing individuals to control prosthetic limbs and even interact with computers using their minds. These technologies may help enhance longevity by addressing physical disabilities caused by aging.

Uploading Consciousness:

The concept of uploading human consciousness to digital substrates, such as computers, is still in the realm of science fiction. However, some researchers in the field of mind uploading believe that it may one day be possible to create a form of "virtual living forever" by transferring human consciousness into a machine.

Cryonics and Biostasis:

Preserving the Body for the Future:

Cryonics involves preserving the human body (or brain) at extremely low temperatures after death, with the hope that future advancements in technology will allow for revival. While cryonics is still controversial and speculative, it has generated significant interest from those hoping to benefit from future breakthroughs in life extension.

Ethical and Practical Challenges:

Critics argue that cryonics raises numerous ethical and logistical concerns, including the uncertainty of revival and the potential risks of future technological failure. Furthermore, questions about the nature of identity and consciousness in the context of revival remain unresolved.

The Pursuit of Biological Longevity:

Extending Healthspan:

The focus of modern longevity research is not only on extending lifespan but also on extending healthspan—the period of life in which an individual remains healthy and free from age-related diseases. This involves lifestyle interventions, pharmacological treatments, and cutting-edge medical therapies.

Human Trials and Experimental Therapies:

Numerous experimental therapies for extending life are now undergoing clinical trials. These treatments, which range from gene therapies to anti-aging drugs, bring us closer to a world where biological living forever could become a reality.

5. Ethical and Philosophical Challenges

Inequity in Access:

Who Gets to Live Forever?:

The potential for living forever raises significant concerns about access and equity. Advanced life-extension technologies may be available only to the wealthy, exacerbating existing social inequalities.

This could lead to a divide between the "immortal" elite and the rest of society.

Global Disparities in Health:

As some people pursue living forever, many others around the world still lack access to basic healthcare. This disparity raises ethical questions about the allocation of resources and the moral implications of investing in living forever technologies when so many basic needs are unmet.

The Value of Mortality:

Meaning and Motivation:

Philosophers have long debated whether living forever would diminish the value of life. If death were no longer inevitable, would life lose its sense of urgency and meaning? Some argue that the finiteness of life gives it purpose and that living forever could undermine the human experience.

Overpopulation Concerns:

Extended lifespans could exacerbate the problem of overpopulation, leading to resource depletion, environmental degradation, and social strain. These concerns pose significant challenges for societies pursuing living forever.

The Psychological Impact:

Living Too Long:

The prospect of living forever could have profound psychological consequences. Some researchers warn that prolonged life may lead to stagnation, boredom, or existential crises as individuals struggle to find new meaning in a world that has changed dramatically over centuries.

Loss of Identity:

Over time, an individual's personal identity may erode as they adapt to changing technologies, cultures, and environments.. The psychological impact of living for centuries or millennia remains an open question.

Lessons from the Scientific Journey

The Interplay of Science and Philosophy:

While Western science focuses on material solutions to aging, integrating thought-provoking and ethical perspectives into the conversation can enrich the pursuit of living forever. A balanced approach that considers the human condition, societal impact, and the meaning of life can help guide the science-focused quest for longevity.

The Importance of Holistic Approaches:

As modern science progresses, it becomes increasingly clear that true longevity requires a holistic approach that integrates mind, body, and spirit. Lessons from ancient wisdom—such as balance, harmony, and community—are just as relevant today as they were in the past. The pursuit of living forever is not only about extending life but also about finding meaning, purpose, and fulfilment in the time we have.

The Western science-focused pursuit of living forever represents humanity's relentless quest to conquer aging and death. While significant progress has been made, the journey raises profound ethical, psychological, and thought-provoking questions. This pursuit is not just about achieving longer life but also about navigating the intriguingities of existence in a world increasingly defined by technological advancement.

Chapter 2

The Science of Immortality

For millennia, human beings have been bound by the biological constraints of aging, disease, and genetic predisposition. Our ancestors viewed aging as inevitable—a force as natural and unstoppable as the passage of time. But in the modern era, science and technology have begun to challenge this ancient paradigm. With the rise of biotechnology, humanity is on the brink of redefining these boundaries.

No longer are we limited to dreams of the "Fountain of Youth" or mystical elixirs. Instead, we wield tools like genetic engineering, regenerative medicine, and precision drug development, each offering profound possibilities for life extension. This chapter explores the leading-edge advancements in biotechnology, revealing how these innovations are driving humanity closer to the age-old dream of living forever.

Understanding the Biological Limits of Aging

Aging is a intriguing biological process that involves the gradual decline of cellular function, energy production, and repair mechanisms. While ancient healers viewed aging as a curse, modern science has demystified its core mechanisms, presenting them as challenges to be overcome rather than immutable laws of nature.

What Is Aging?

Cellular Senescence:

Every cell in the human body has a limited capacity for division. Over time, as cells accumulate damage from stress, toxins, and mutations, they enter a state called senescence, where they no longer divide. Senescent cells emit inflammatory signals, accelerating the aging process and increasing the risk of chronic diseases like cancer, diabetes, and cardiovascular disease.

Telomere Shortening:

Telomeres are protective caps at the ends of chromosomes that act as "biological clocks" for cellular division. Each time a cell divides, its telomeres shorten. When the telomeres become too short, the cell enters senescence or undergoes programmed cell death (apoptosis).

Mitochondrial Decline:

The mitochondria, often called the "powerhouses" of cells, convert food into energy. Over time, mitochondrial DNA accumulates damage from free radicals, leading to reduced energy production and cellular dysfunction. This energy deficit plays a significant role in aging-related diseases, including neurodegeneration.

The Concept of a Biological Ceiling:

The Hayflick Limit:

In 1961, scientist Leonard Hayflick discovered that human cells can only divide about 40-60 times before becoming senescent. This concept, known as the Hayflick limit, established that cellular lifespan is finite—a biological "ceiling" that scientists now seek to break.

Caloric Restriction and Lifespan:

Research has shown that reducing caloric intake in animals extends their lifespan. This occurs due to the activation of stress-response pathways that enhance cellular repair and longevity. The concept has inspired human "biohackers" to adopt fasting protocols in hopes of reaping similar benefits.

Biotechnology's Role in Extending Lifespan

Biotechnology has reimagined the fight against aging, moving from treatment to prevention—and perhaps even reversal. Emerging tools are allowing scientists to rewrite genetic instructions, restore cellular health, and slow or reverse the damage that accumulates over time.

Genetic Engineering and Longevity:

CRISPR and Gene Editing:

CRISPR is a revolutionary gene-editing tool that allows for precise modifications of DNA. By removing, adding, or altering specific genes, scientists can eliminate genetic predispositions to aging-related diseases. For example, the FOXO3 gene, which is linked to longevity, is being studied for potential gene-editing interventions.

Epigenetic Reprogramming:

Our genes are influenced by epigenetic markers—chemical tags that determine which genes are active or inactive. By "reprogramming" these markers, scientists aim to return aged cells to a more youthful state. Researcher Dr. David Sinclair's work on Yamanaka factors has shown that it's possible to partially "rejuvenate" cells by resetting their epigenetic state.

Regenerative Medicine:

Stem Cell Therapy:

Stem cells have the unique ability to transform into any cell type in the body. By using stem cell infusions, scientists can regenerate aging tissues and reverse damage caused by injury, disease, or age. Clinical trials have shown promise in treating heart disease, neurodegeneration, and even vision loss.

3D Bioprinting:

Imagine a future where you can "print" a new liver, kidney, or heart on demand. With 3D bioprinting, human tissues and organs are being produced using living cells as "bio-ink." This could eliminate organ transplant waiting lists and extend human lifespan by providing replacement parts for failing organs.

Addressing Cellular Senescence:

Senolytics:

Senolytics are a new class of drugs designed to eliminate senescent cells. By clearing these "zombie cells" from the body, tissues can function more efficiently, reducing inflammation and delaying age-related diseases. Early trials on dasatinib and quercetin have shown significant healthspan improvements in mice.

NAD+ Boosters:

NAD+ (Nicotinamide Adenine Dinucleotide) is a coenzyme essential for energy production and DNA repair. As we age, NAD+ levels decline. Supplements like NR (nicotinamide riboside) and

NMN (nicotinamide mononucleotide) aim to restore these levels, potentially improving metabolism and reducing signs of aging.

Synthetic Biology and Redefining Life

While traditional biotechnology focuses on "editing" existing life, synthetic biology aims to build life from scratch. This field could revolutionize human health, allowing us to design custom cells, organs, and even entirely new organisms.

Artificial Cells:

Scientists are creating synthetic cells that mimic human cells. These "programmable" cells could one day replace malfunctioning tissues or serve as "biological computers" within the body, detecting and repairing damage.

Horizontal Gene Transfer:

Inspired by how bacteria transfer genes among themselves, scientists are exploring the possibility of inserting beneficial traits from other species into human genomes. Imagine having the regenerative capacity of a jellyfish or the longevity of a tortoise.

Targeting the Root Causes of Aging

While earlier efforts sought to delay the symptoms of aging, modern approaches aim to target the root causes. This shift represents a strategic pivot from managing disease to truly combating the biological underpinnings of mortality.

Telomere Extension:

Inserting the enzyme telomerase into human cells can extend telomeres, allowing cells to divide beyond the Hayflick limit. Studies have shown that telomerase therapy extends lifespan in mice, though safety concerns remain for human applications.

Mitochondrial Enhancement:

Mitochondrial replacement therapy replaces faulty mitochondria with healthy ones, offering a strategy to treat mitochondrial diseases. Other approaches involve stimulating mitophagy—the process by which cells "clean up" damaged mitochondria.

Microbiome Modulation:

Our gut microbiome significantly impacts health and longevity. By optimizing gut bacteria through diet, probiotics, and prebiotics, researchers aim to reduce inflammation, support immunity, and slow aging.

Biotechnological Innovations on the Horizon

The Longevity Economy:

Startups like Calico (funded by Google) and Altos Labs (backed by Jeff Bezos) are investing billions in longevity research. Their mission is simple but ambitious: to delay, prevent, or even reverse aging.

Cryonics and Biostasis:

Cryonics involves freezing human bodies after death with the hope of future revival. While it remains controversial, advances in tissue vitrification are improving the feasibility of preserving organs and bodies for long-term storage.

Ethical and Practical Challenges

While the promise of living forever is alluring, it raises ethical and practical concerns that must be addressed.

Access and Inequality:

Will life-extension technologies only be available to the wealthy? If so, society risks creating a "longevity divide" where only the rich can afford to live longer.

Overpopulation:

What happens if billions of people live for centuries? Humanity may face new challenges in resource allocation, housing, and employment.

Psychological Impact:

How will individuals grapple with the idea of living for centuries or millennia? Some philosophers argue that finite life is what gives life meaning.

A Balanced Perspective

The science of living forever is not just a technical journey—it's a profound reflection on what it means to be human. While biotechnology offers extraordinary potential for longer, healthier lives, it also compels us to confront deeper questions about equity, purpose, and identity.

In the end, the goal may not be to live forever, but to live more fully, with health, vitality, and meaning—no matter how long the journey lasts.

Regenerative Medicine: Can We Reverse Aging?

For centuries, the dream of reversing aging seemed confined to the realm of mythology and science fiction. But today, regenerative medicine stands at the forefront of making this dream a tangible reality. By repairing, replacing, or regenerating damaged cells, tissues, and organs, this revolutionary field promises to redefine human health and longevity.

Fuelled by breakthroughs in stem cell research, tissue engineering, and gene therapy, regenerative medicine doesn't just aim to slow down aging — it strives to turn back the biological clock. This chapter explores the principles, advances, and profound implications of regenerative medicine for human health, offering a glimpse into a future where age may no longer define us.

Understanding Aging at the Cellular Level

Aging begins at the cellular level, where the body's natural repair systems gradually lose efficiency. By understanding the root causes of aging, regenerative medicine seeks to restore these mechanisms and even reverse their effects.

Cellular Senescence:

What is Cellular Senescence? Cells lose their ability to divide and function, entering a state of dormancy. This process prevents cancerous growth but has a downside — senescent cells accumulate and release inflammatory molecules that contribute to aging and age-related diseases.

Impact on Aging:

The buildup of senescent cells causes organ dysfunction, impairs tissue repair, and accelerates the development of diseases like Alzheimer's, arthritis, and cardiovascular conditions.

Tissue Regeneration Limits:

Decline in Stem Cells:

The body's supply of adult stem cells, which are crucial for tissue repair, declines in number and efficiency as we age.

Loss of Regenerative Capacity:

Tissues lose their ability to heal from damage, making it harder for the body to recover from injury or illness.

Principles of Regenerative Medicine

The core idea of regenerative medicine is to restore the body's innate ability to heal. This is achieved through key pillars like stem cells, tissue engineering, and gene therapy.

Stem Cells: The Building Blocks of Regeneration:

Types of Stem Cells:

Embryonic Stem Cells (ESCs):

Can develop into any type of tissue but raise ethical concerns.

Adult Stem Cells:

Found in specific tissues like bone marrow, but their potential is more limited than ESCs.

Induced Pluripotent Stem Cells (iPSCs):

Mature cells reprogrammed to mimic ESCs, offering immense potential without ethical *issues.*

Therapeutic Potential:

Stem cells can regenerate damaged tissues, offering new hope for diseases like Parkinson's, Alzheimer's, and heart disease.

Tissue Engineering:

Scaffolds and Bioprinting:

3D bioprinting technology creates "scaffolds" to guide the growth of tissues and organs.

Applications:

Artificial skin for burn victims, cartilage for arthritis patients, and lab-grown organs like kidneys and hearts for transplants.

Gene Therapy:

Editing the Blueprint:

With tools like CRISPR, scientists can edit genes to correct genetic defects that cause aging-related diseases.

Gene Delivery Systems:

Viral vectors and nanoparticles deliver therapeutic genes to target cells, helping to trigger regenerative effects.

Breakthroughs in Reversing Aging

As science advances, once-theoretical concepts are turning into practical, life-altering treatments.

Removing Senescent Cells:

Senolytics:

Drugs like dasatinib and quercetin selectively remove senescent cells, reducing inflammation and promoting tissue repair.

Clinical Progress:

Animal studies have shown improved physical function, reduced frailty, and increased lifespan. Human clinical trials are underway.

Telomere Lengthening:

Telomeres and Cellular Lifespan:

Telomeres are the protective caps on the ends of chromosomes. Every time a cell divides, these caps shorten until the cell can no longer divide.

Telomerase Activation:

By reactivating the enzyme telomerase, researchers have extended telomeres in animal studies, delaying the aging process.

Rejuvenation through Epigenetic Reprogramming:

Epigenetics and Aging:

While our DNA remains unchanged, gene expression is altered as we age. This can be reversed.

Yamanaka Factors:

Named after Nobel laureate Shinya Yamanaka, these four genes can reprogram cells to a "younger" state. Animal studies suggest that introducing these factors could rejuvenate entire organs.

Regenerative Therapies in Practice

The field of regenerative medicine is no longer just theoretical. It is already impacting healthcare and changing lives.

Regenerating Organs:

Lab-Grown Organs:

Scientists are growing human organs like kidneys and hearts using stem cells and bioprinting technology.

Transplant Revolution:

Custom-grown organs may eliminate the need for donors, reduce transplant rejection, and solve the organ shortage crisis.

Treating Age-Related Diseases:

Neurological Conditions:

Stem cell therapy is being explored for Alzheimer's, Parkinson's, and spinal cord injuries.

Cardiovascular Regeneration:

Following heart attacks, stem cells and tissue patches are used to regenerate damaged heart tissue.

Extending Healthspan, Not Just Lifespan:

Focus on Quality of Life:

The goal is not just to live longer, but to live better — reducing frailty, restoring mobility, and enhancing overall vitality.

The Future of Regenerative Medicine

Looking ahead, the boundaries of regenerative medicine continue to expand, offering possibilities once considered science fiction.

Whole-Body Rejuvenation:

Systemic Approaches:

Instead of treating one part of the body, researchers are working on techniques to rejuvenate entire systems, like the immune system or circulatory system.

Parabiosis Studies:

Studies in which old animals receive blood from young animals have shown signs of rejuvenation, though the ethical implications are being debated.

Cryonics and Biostasis:

Preserving for the Future:

Advances in cryopreservation technology may allow tissues, organs, or entire bodies to be frozen and revived later. While still speculative, this concept is receiving increased attention.

Personalized Regeneration:

Precision Medicine:

By tailoring regenerative therapies to a person's unique genetic profile, doctors can deliver highly personalized, more effective treatments.

Bioinformatics and AI:

AI models are being used to predict how regenerative therapies will interact with a person's biology, leading to safer, more targeted treatments.

Ethical and Social Considerations

With the power to reverse aging comes significant ethical and societal challenges.

Equity of Access:

Healthcare Disparities:

Regenerative therapies are costly, which could lead to "longevity inequality," where only the rich can afford to live longer, healthier lives.

Global Disparities:

Wealthy countries may benefit from these advances first, leaving developing countries behind.

Overpopulation and Resource Strain:

Sustainability Challenges:

If lifespans increase significantly, global resource shortages, environmental stress, and economic strain may arise.

The Psychological Toll:

Living in a Young Body Forever:

While living in a youthful state sounds appealing, the psychological challenges of an "ageless" existence are unknown. Will people experience existential boredom, loss of purpose, or shifts in relationships?

A New Era of Longevity

Regenerative medicine is redefining what it means to grow old. From stem cells and tissue engineering to ground-breaking gene therapies, the possibility of reversing aging has never been more real. These advances promise not only to add years to life but to add life to those years, improving vitality and health span.

However, this journey is not without its moral and social intriguingities. Who will have access to these treatments? How will humanity deal with the consequences of longer lifespans? And how will our sense of purpose evolve if we live to 150 or beyond?

Regenerative medicine invites us to reimagine human life itself. As science and spirituality converge, we may be on the brink of transcending our biological limits — a future where aging is not a certainty but a choice.

The Role of Stem Cells and Genetic Engineering

Unlocking the Blueprint of Life:

At the intersection of biotechnology and medicine, stem cells and genetic engineering are rewriting the story of human biology, health, and aging. What once seemed like the stuff of science fiction — regenerating organs, reversing aging, and enhancing human abilities — is now becoming reality. These two revolutionary forces offer the potential to repair tissues, combat genetic disorders, and perhaps even unlock the secret to living forever.

Stem cells, often called the "architects of regeneration," possess the unique ability to transform into various cell types. Genetic engineering, on the other hand, enables scientists to edit the human genome with precision, altering our genetic "blueprint" to enhance health and longevity. Together, they form a powerful duo that could extend lifespan, enhance healthspan, and redefine the very nature of aging.

This section delves into the transformative role of stem cells and genetic engineering, exploring their potential, challenges, and future implications for humanity's quest to overcome the limits of biology.

Stem Cells: The Architects of Regeneration

What Are Stem Cells?

Stem cells are the body's "raw materials" — undifferentiated cells capable of self-renewal and transforming into specialized cells. Their regenerative potential makes them indispensable for growth, repair, and healing.

Types of Stem Cells:

Embryonic Stem Cells (ESCs):

Pluripotent cells derived from early-stage embryos, capable of forming any type of cell in the body.

Adult Stem Cells (ASCs):

Found in tissues like bone marrow, with a more limited capacity to differentiate but still crucial for repair and maintenance.

Induced Pluripotent Stem Cells (iPSCs):

Mature cells that are "reprogrammed" to behave like ESCs, bypassing ethical issues and offering vast therapeutic potential.

Applications in Longevity:

Stem cells are at the heart of regenerative medicine, with profound implications for longevity.

Tissue Repair and Regeneration:

Stem cells can regenerate damaged organs like the heart, liver, and kidneys, offering hope for treating age-related organ failure.

Neurodegenerative Diseases:

Stem cell therapy aims to restore neurons lost in conditions like Alzheimer's, Parkinson's, and spinal cord injuries.

Skin and Cosmetic Regeneration:

Stem cells are increasingly used in aesthetic medicine to rejuvenate aging skin, reduce wrinkles, and repair damaged tissue.

Advancements in Stem Cell Technology:

Innovations in stem cell technology are pushing the boundaries of what is possible.

Organoid Cultures:

Miniature, lab-grown "organs in a dish" allow researchers to study disease mechanisms and test treatments.

Stem Cell Banking:

Individuals are now banking stem cells from their own bodies, preserving them for future regenerative treatments.

Genetic Engineering: Editing Life's Blueprint

What Is Genetic Engineering?

Genetic engineering involves modifying an organism's DNA to change its characteristics. By "rewriting" the genetic code, scientists can eliminate diseases, enhance traits, or even delay aging.

Key Techniques in Genetic Engineering:

CRISPR-Cas9:

A revolutionary gene-editing tool that allows precise "cut-and-paste" edits to DNA, enabling scientists to correct genetic defects.

Gene Therapy:

The introduction of therapeutic genes into cells to replace faulty or missing genes, often via viral vectors.

Applications in Longevity:

By altering the genes that regulate aging and longevity, genetic engineering holds the key to extending lifespan.

Eliminating Genetic Disorders:

CRISPR can be used to correct DNA mutations responsible for genetic diseases, extending both lifespan and healthspan.

Targeting Aging-Related Genes:

FOXO3 and SIRT Genes: These genes are associated with longevity and are being studied for their potential to slow aging.

Telomere Maintenance:

Telomeres, protective caps on chromosomes, shorten as we age. By genetically preserving telomeres, scientists aim to delay cellular aging.

Improving Cellular Efficiency:

By modifying mitochondrial DNA, genetic engineering could enhance energy production and reduce oxidative stress, a key contributor to aging.

Synthetic Biology and Designer Genes:

Synthetic biology takes genetic engineering a step further, creating entirely new genetic "designs" to optimize organisms.

Creating Optimized Organisms:

Using computer-aided design, scientists can create organisms with enhanced traits, such as disease resistance or extended lifespans.

Biohacking Longevity:

Citizen scientists are experimenting with self-administered genetic modifications to slow aging, though this remains controversial and risky.

The Synergy of Stem Cells and Genetic Engineering

Stem cells and genetic engineering don't operate in isolation. When combined, their potential multiplies, opening doors to new regenerative therapies.

Reprogramming Aging Cells:

The synergy between stem cells and genetic engineering enables cellular rejuvenation.

Yamanaka Factors:

By introducing four key genes, adult cells can be "reset" to a youthful, pluripotent state, effectively reversing the effects of aging.

Epigenetic Reprogramming:

Gene expression can be modified without changing the underlying DNA sequence, restoring cell function and slowing the aging process.

Personalized Medicine:

With stem cells and genetic engineering, medical treatments can be personalized to an individual's unique genetic makeup.

Tailored Therapies:

Stem cells and edited genes can be customized to suit each patient's genetic and cellular profile.

Disease Prevention:

Edited stem cells can be preloaded with protective genes, making them more resilient to age-related diseases before being transplanted into the body.

Enhancing Regenerative Potential:

Super Stem Cells:

By genetically engineering stem cells to resist inflammation or enhance their differentiation potential, researchers are creating "super" versions with enhanced regenerative capacity.

Current Challenges and Ethical Considerations

As with any powerful technology, stem cells and genetic engineering come with ethical, technical, and social challenges.

Ethical Dilemmas:

Embryonic Stem Cell Debate:

The use of ESCs raises ethical questions about the destruction of embryos, leading to a shift toward iPSC technology.

Designer Babies:

While genetic engineering can prevent disease, it also raises concerns about non-medical enhancements, like altering intelligence or physical traits.

Technical Challenges:

Delivery Mechanisms:

Efficiently delivering edited genes or stem cells to target tissues remains a challenge.

Immune Rejection:

Transplanted cells or genes may be rejected by the body, requiring further innovation to ensure compatibility.

Accessibility and Equity:

Cost of Therapies:

Advanced treatments are expensive, raising concerns about access and affordability.

Global Access:

Ensuring these technologies are accessible to all — not just the wealthy — will be a critical issue in the coming decades.

Future Horizons

The future of stem cells and genetic engineering is filled with promise, with researchers exploring bold new possibilities.

Whole-Body Rejuvenation:

Systemic Interventions:

By combining stem cell infusions with genetic therapies, researchers aim to rejuvenate entire organ systems.

Parabiosis Research:

The transfusion of young blood into older individuals has shown signs of rejuvenation, though the science remains controversial.

Aging as a Treatable Condition:

FDA-Approved Therapies:

New therapies are being developed that treat aging as a medical condition rather than an inevitable decline.

Aging Biomarkers:

Tracking genetic and cellular changes allows researchers to measure the effectiveness of anti-aging treatments in real time.

The Role of Artificial Intelligence (AI)

AI is accelerating the development of stem cell and genetic engineering technologies.

Accelerating Research:

AI algorithms analyze genetic data to identify longevity targets faster than traditional methods.

Optimizing Therapies:

Machine learning models predict the best combinations of stem cell and gene-editing treatments for specific individuals.

Redefining What It Means to Be Human

The fusion of stem cells and genetic engineering represents a profound shift in human history. What once seemed impossible — reversing aging, curing genetic diseases, and enhancing human potential — is now within reach.

While challenges remain, the promise of these technologies is undeniable. Stem cells can rebuild organs, repair tissues, and rejuvenate the body, while genetic engineering offers the chance to correct our biological flaws at the source. Together, they could fundamentally alter the human experience, allowing people to live longer, healthier, and more vibrant lives.

But with great power comes great responsibility. Ethical questions about equity, fairness, and human identity loom large. Will these technologies be accessible to all, or only to a privileged few? How will living longer affect our sense of purpose and identity?

As humanity stands on the cusp of a new era, the role of stem cells and genetic engineering in our collective future has never been more significant. These technologies invite us to reimagine not just how we live, but what it means to be human.

The Future of Human Enhancement: Trans humanism and Beyond

Redefining Human Boundaries:

The human desire to transcend physical, mental, and existential limitations has driven progress for millennia. Today, this quest extends beyond medicine and biology into the uncharted territory of technological integration and human enhancement. Central to this pursuit is transhumanism, a movement that envisions a future where human beings evolve beyond their natural state through advanced technologies.

This movement challenges our deepest assumptions about life, death, and what it means to be human. By enhancing our bodies, minds, and consciousness, transhumanism promises to not only extend lifespan but also to break free from the constraints of disease, aging, and even mortality. This chapter explores the core tenets of transhumanism, its technological pathways, societal impact, and what lies beyond the horizon of human evolution.

Understanding Transhumanism

The Core Philosophy:

At its heart, trans humanism is about overcoming human limitations. By merging biology with advanced technology, trans humanists aim to achieve a future where human potential is no longer bound by genetics, biology, or fate. The movement envisions a world where humanity evolves into a "post-human" state, marked by increased intelligence, physical prowess, and psychological resilience.

Key Pathways of Enhancement:

Biological Augmentation: Using genetic engineering, regenerative medicine, and cellular reprogramming to enhance physical abilities, health, and lifespan.

Technological Integration: Merging the human body with AI, robotics, brain-computer interfaces (BCIs), and nanotechnology to augment cognitive abilities, sensory perception, and overall performance.

Historical Context:

The thought-provoking roots of trans humanism trace back to influential thinkers who dreamed of transcending human nature.

Friedrich Nietzsche's Übermensch:

The concept of the "overman" (Übermensch) reflects an ideal being who overcomes human frailty, embodying strength, willpower, and self-mastery.

Julian Huxley:

The 20th-century biologist and philosopher coined the term "trans humanism," envisioning a world where humans, through science and reason, overcome their biological limits.

These thought-provoking visions have since evolved into a technological agenda that embraces artificial intelligence, gene editing, and digital living forever as tools for human transformation.

Technological Pathways to Human Enhancement

Cognitive Enhancements:

If the mind defines human identity, then enhancing cognitive abilities is one of transhumanism's most profound goals. Advances in brain-machine interfaces (BCIs) and AI-assisted learning could revolutionize how we think, learn, and connect with each other.

Key Innovations:

Neuroprosthetics and Brain-Computer Interfaces (BCIs):

Projects like Elon Musk's Neuralink aim to link the human brain with computers, enabling memory enhancement, direct mind-to-machine communication, and even the possibility of telepathic interaction.

AI-Assisted Learning:

AI-driven education systems can tailor learning experiences to individual cognitive needs, significantly enhancing intellectual capacity and creativity.

Physical Augmentation:

Transhumanism also seeks to transform the physical body, turning humans into more durable, efficient, and adaptable beings.

Key Innovations:

Exoskeletons and Robotics: Wearable robotic suits boost strength, endurance, and mobility, offering hope for the elderly, disabled, and military personnel.

Nanotechnology: Microscopic nanobots could roam the bloodstream, repairing tissues, eliminating toxins, and maintaining cellular health in real time.

Genetic Engineering: Tools like CRISPR-Cas9 enable precise editing of genes, allowing for enhanced immune systems, resistance to diseases, and even physical attributes like improved muscle mass or skin regeneration.

Digital Immortality:

What if consciousness itself could be preserved, even after the body decays? The idea of “mind uploading” proposes just that — digitizing human consciousness to exist in non-biological substrates.

Key Innovations:

Mind Uploading: Companies like Nectome aim to preserve the brain's structure for potential digitization, with the ultimate goal of transferring consciousness to a digital platform.

Augmented Reality (AR) and Virtual Reality (VR): AR and VR environments could offer a form of "virtual living forever," where digital versions of people live on as interactive simulations.

Ethical and Societal Implications

Ethical Challenges:

Trans humanism forces us to confront deep ethical dilemmas about identity, equity, and the essence of humanity.

Redefining Humanity:

If enhancements allow people to become "superhuman," will enhanced individuals still be considered human, or something new altogether?

Access and Equity:

Will access to these enhancements be limited to the wealthy, creating a new class of "enhanced" elite, while the rest are left behind?

Informed Consent:

As technologies like BCIs and gene editing become available, ensuring people fully understand the long-term consequences of these modifications will be critical.

Societal Impact:

Beyond right and wrong, transhumanist technologies will likely alter the fabric of society itself.

Redefining Work and Productivity:

Enhanced humans with superior cognitive and physical abilities may dominate the workforce, displacing unenhanced workers and widening economic inequalities.

New Social Classes:

If access to enhancements is unequal, humanity could fracture into new "classes" of enhanced versus natural humans, exacerbating social divisions.

Beyond Transhumanism: The Post-Human Future

The Concept of Post-Humanism:

While transhumanism seeks to enhance human capabilities, post-humanism goes further, envisioning beings that are no longer "human" by any traditional definition. These beings may be digital minds, synthetic organisms, or hybrids of human consciousness and AI.

Key Possibilities:

Synthetic Beings: Human consciousness could merge with robotics or AI to create "post-human" entities that are no longer limited by biological constraints.

Collective Intelligence: Enhanced minds could form interconnected "hive minds," allowing people to share thoughts and ideas directly, creating a form of super-intelligence.

Ecosystem Integration: Post-humans may achieve seamless integration with the natural environment, using technology to achieve sustainable coexistence with nature.

Cosmic Longevity:

The pursuit of living forever may extend beyond Earth, as transhumanist enhancements enable humans to survive in space.

Space Colonization:

Enhanced physiology, stronger immunity, and resistance to cosmic radiation could enable human survival on Mars or other planets.

Astrobiological Adaptations:

Genetic modifications may allow humans to adapt to the unique conditions of alien environments, enabling survival in extreme climates.

Current Developments and Future Directions

Advances in Human-Machine Symbiosis:

Emerging technologies are rapidly making the concept of "human-machine symbiosis" a reality.

Notable Developments:

AI Collaboration: AI systems are helping scientists design and test transhumanist technologies faster and more efficiently.

Wearable Enhancements: Smartwatches, AR glasses, and wearable health monitors are early signs of a broader movement toward human-machine convergence.

Philosophical and Spiritual Perspectives:

While transhumanism is often viewed as a technological movement, it also raises questions about spirituality and consciousness.

Key Concepts:

Integrating Technology and Spirituality:

Some argue that technological advancements can amplify human spirituality, offering new pathways to enlightenment and inner growth.

Eternal Consciousness:

If consciousness can be uploaded and preserved digitally, what does it mean for the concept of "soul" or "afterlife"?

Embracing a New Frontier of Humanity

As the lines between human, machine, and AI blur, transhumanism and post-humanism challenge us to confront our deepest fears and hopes. Are we willing to abandon biological constraints in pursuit of a "better" version of ourselves? Will living forever be a blessing or a curse?

The ethical and thought-provoking implications are profound. The potential for social stratification, the meaning of human identity, and the impact of digital consciousness all demand thoughtful reflection. If humanity evolves into a network of enhanced beings and disembodied minds, what will "being human" even mean?

One thing is certain: the future of human enhancement will not be a passive journey. It will require bold choices, profound ethical debates, and a shared vision of a world where technology uplifts all of humanity, not just a privileged few. The fusion of flesh, mind, and machine offers a tantalizing vision of living forever — one where humanity may finally transcend death, not through divine intervention, but through the force of its own ingenuity.

As we navigate this frontier, we must ask not only "Can we do it?" but also "Should we?"

Chapter 3
The Ethics of Immortality

The Profound Questions at the Heart of Immortality

Humanity stands at a defining crossroads. What was once the stuff of mythology — the dream of living forever — is rapidly becoming a plausible reality. No longer confined to ancient legends or thought-provoking musings, the pursuit of eternal life is now driven by ground breaking advancements in genetic engineering, AI-driven consciousness preservation, and regenerative medicine. But with this shift comes a far more urgent and unsettling question: "Should we do it?"

While the science-focused community continues its relentless pursuit of life extension, society faces an equally important challenge — grappling with the moral, social, and ecological consequences of this pursuit. What happens when the cycle of life and death, which has governed existence for millennia, is broken? What does it mean to live forever, and more importantly, who gets to live forever?

Unlike other technological advancements, living forever isn't just a matter of science-focused "progress." It touches on deeply human questions about fairness, justice, and the essence of life itself. Who will have access to it? Will living forever become a luxury reserved for the wealthiest elite, or will it be seen as a basic human right, available to all regardless of wealth or status? What happens to the natural balance of the planet when people no longer die at the same rate they are born? Can Earth sustain a world where death is no longer a necessity?

Beneath these societal and ecological concerns lies an even more fundamental question: Is it morally right to defy nature? For thousands of years, mortality has been a universal constant — a force that defines the human experience. Religions, philosophies, and cultural traditions have taught us to accept death as part of life's cycle, giving it purpose and urgency. But what if death was no longer inevitable? What if the "end" was postponed indefinitely? Are we prepared for a world where "forever" is no longer a poetic idea but an actual possibility?

These questions aren't distant, futuristic speculations. They are immediate, pressing ethical dilemmas that demand attention today. As scientists push the boundaries of biology and technology, policymakers, philosophers, and everyday citizens must confront the implications of a world where living forever is within reach. How we answer these questions will not only shape the trajectory of human history but also redefine our understanding of what it means to be alive.

This chapter explores these profound ethical dilemmas through four key perspectives:

- The Morality of Extending Life: Who Deserves to Live Forever?
- The Economic Divide: Access to Immortality Technologies
- The Ecological Impact: Overpopulation and Sustainability
- The Ethical Dilemma: Is Immortality Against Nature?

Each section delves into a different facet of the living forever debate, drawing on insights from philosophy, religion, sociology, and science. Together, they reveal a future that is as exciting as it is unsettling — a future where life, death, and morality must be reimagined from the ground up.

This chapter does not offer easy answers. Instead, it invites readers to reflect deeply on the choices we must make as a species. If the tools for living forever become available, will we wield them wisely, or will we repeat the mistakes of the past? The search for living forever is not just about extending human life — it's about redefining what it means to live.

The Morality of Extending Life: Who Deserves to Live Forever?

As humanity stands at the edge of conquering mortality, a profound ethical dilemma confronts us: Who deserves to live forever? While science races ahead with breakthroughs in genetic engineering, regenerative medicine, and AI-driven consciousness preservation, society must pause to ask: Should everyone have access to living forever, or should it be reserved for those deemed "worthy" by some criteria?

This question is not merely academic. It touches on the essence of fairness, justice, and human dignity. Should eternal life be a universal human right, accessible to all, like clean water and healthcare? Or should it be a privilege for the select few — the wealthy, the powerful, or those who have "earned" it?

This section delves into these difficult moral and thought-provoking questions. It explores the potential frameworks for determining access to living forever, the consequences of inequality, and the role of religion and morality in defining "worthiness."

Should Immortality Be a Universal Right or a Privilege?

At the heart of this debate lies the question of justice and fairness. If humanity possesses the technology to extend life indefinitely, who should have access to it?

One school of thought argues that living forever should be a universal human right, similar to basic healthcare or education. The rationale is simple: If death can be prevented, why should anyone be denied the chance to avoid it? From this perspective, access to living forever should be seen as a fundamental right, regardless of wealth, status, or achievements. Denying someone access to living forever could be viewed as an act of injustice — a violation of the most basic right of all: the right to live.

On the other side of the argument is the view that living forever should be a privilege, not a right. Proponents of this perspective point out that resources such as healthcare, education, and wealth are already distributed unequally. They argue that life extension should follow a similar logic: those who contribute the most to society should be rewarded with the opportunity to live longer. Innovators, thought leaders, and high-impact individuals could be prioritized for access, as their continued existence could accelerate human progress.

Key Ethical Questions

- Should living forever be a universal right or a merit-based privilege?

- If it is a privilege, what criteria should be used to determine eligibility?
- Should individuals with criminal histories or unethical behaviour be disqualified from access to living forever?

Philosophical Lens:

Utilitarian Perspective:

From a utilitarian standpoint, the goal is to maximize overall well-being. This might justify prioritizing living forever for individuals who can contribute the most to society's welfare.

Deontological Perspective:

A deontological approach, which emphasizes fairness and equality, would argue that living forever should be available to all, regardless of their societal contributions or moral status.

Meritocracy and Immortality: Who "Deserves" to Live Forever?

If living forever is not a universal right, but rather a selective opportunity, society must ask: What makes someone "deserving" of living forever?

In modern societies, access to opportunities like jobs, scholarships, and promotions is often based on meritocracy. Those who work hard, excel, or contribute significantly are given greater rewards. If this logic is extended to living forever, one might argue that certain people — scientists, thinkers, humanitarians, and innovators — have "earned" the right to live longer.

Possible Criteria for "Deserving" Immortality:

Intellectual Contributions: Those who have contributed to human knowledge (scientists, inventors, and innovators) may be seen as deserving because their continued existence benefits humanity as a whole.

Humanitarian Contributions: People who dedicate their lives to helping others — philanthropists, activists, and social reformers — might be viewed as more deserving of living forever than those who live selfishly.

Moral Character: Should good behaviour be a requirement for living forever? If so, how do we define "good"? Would those who engage in selfish or unethical behaviour be excluded?

While meritocracy may seem fair on the surface, it introduces subjective judgments and risks bias and discrimination. Who decides what counts as "merit"? What happens to those who are deemed "unworthy"? History shows that when humans are given power to decide "worthiness," oppression follows. If life-extension technology is controlled by the elite, it could create a system where the rich live forever, and the poor are condemned to mortality.

Key Ethical Questions

- Is it ethical to base access to living forever on merit?
- If merit-based access is allowed, who defines "merit" and how?
- Will a merit-based system create an "immortal elite" with too much power?

Philosophical Lens:

Rawlsian Perspective:

Philosopher John Rawls argued for justice based on the "veil of ignorance," where social policies should be designed as if people didn't know their own social position. From this perspective, granting living forever only to the "deserving" would be unjust, as no one would willingly accept being part of the excluded class.

Aristotelian Perspective:

Aristotle emphasized the pursuit of eudaimonia (human flourishing) as the purpose of life. From this perspective, those who actively contribute to the flourishing of humanity could be seen as worthy of a longer life.

Immortality and Social Inequality: The Risks of a New Elite Class

If life-extension technology is only available to the wealthy, we risk creating a biological caste system. Imagine a world where the rich live forever, while the poor face the inevitability of death. Such a scenario raises questions about economic justice and power imbalance.

We already live in a world where healthcare, education, and opportunity are unequally distributed. If living forever follows the same trend, the rich may become a biologically immortal elite with vast control over society. Wealth would compound across generations, as immortal families accumulate power, property, and influence. Intergenerational mobility would stagnate, as the young are denied the opportunities held by immortal leaders.

Potential Consequences of Inequality:

Eternal Dynasties: Families of immortals could amass wealth and influence across centuries, becoming an entrenched elite.

Social Unrest: The gap between the "immortal elite" and the "mortal masses" could trigger social rebellion, unrest, and revolution.

Stagnation of Innovation: If those in power live forever, they may resist new ideas, stifling creativity, innovation, and cultural evolution.

Key Ethical Questions:

- How do we prevent a future of "immortal elites" and "mortal underclasses"?
- Should governments regulate access to living forever to ensure fairness?
- Can society prevent the formation of an "eternal ruling class"?

Philosophical Lens:

Marxist Perspective:

Marxists might see living forever as a form of "biological capital" that allows the rich to oppress the poor. Calls for collective ownership of life-extension technology would likely follow.

Utilitarian Perspective:

Utilitarians may argue for a system that prioritizes those who can produce the greatest societal benefit, even if that means inequality.

The Role of Religion and Morality in Defining Worthiness

For millennia, human spirituality and religion have shaped our understanding of life and death. Many religious traditions teach that mortality is part of the divine order, and tampering with it may be seen as "playing God." If living forever becomes a technological reality, what role will religious morality play in deciding worthiness?

Some religious leaders may argue that no human is "worthy" of living forever except through divine grace. Religious texts often emphasize humility and submission to a higher power, and the pursuit of living forever may be seen as an act of hubris.

Key Ethical Questions:

- Should religious beliefs shape access to living forever?
- If religious groups reject living forever, should society respect their right to refuse it?
- How do we balance technological progress with spiritual values?

Philosophical Lens:

Existentialist Perspective: Existentialists like Kierkegaard argue that life's meaning comes from the acceptance of mortality. If living forever becomes possible, the existential framework of human life may collapse.

Theological Perspective: Many religious worldviews see life and death as part of the divine plan. If technology disrupts this plan, it could challenge long-held spiritual and moral beliefs.

The morality of extending life forces us to confront the essence of what it means to be human. Whether living forever is framed as a right, a privilege, or a reward will shape the future of humanity. Our answers will decide if we create a world of equality and shared progress or one of immortal elites and mortal underclasses. The question of "who deserves to live forever" reflects our deepest beliefs about justice, fairness, and the purpose of human existence.

The Economic Divide: Access to Immortality Technologies

As humanity edges closer to unlocking the secrets of living forever, a profound and uncomfortable question emerges: Who will be able to afford it? While the notion of eternal life has long been the domain of mythology and religion, it is now on the verge of becoming a tangible reality, thanks to breakthroughs in gene editing, AI-driven consciousness transfers, and anti-aging therapies. But if history serves as a guide, access to this monumental advancement may not be equal.

From organ transplants to cancer immunotherapy, access to life-saving technology has often been determined by wealth. The early stages of most ground breaking innovations follow a predictable pattern: privilege first, equality later — if at all. Will the dream of living forever follow the same path? If so, humanity could see the rise of a world where the wealthy live indefinitely while the rest of society faces mortality as an inescapable fate.

This section explores the possible consequences of an economic divide in access to living forever technologies. It addresses the cost of living forever, the rise of a biological caste system, and potential solutions such as universal access models, government regulation, and public ownership of key technologies.

The Cost of Immortality: A Tale of Economic Inequality

The race toward living forever is not a solo sprint but a relay involving scientists, corporations, and venture capitalists. Developing life-extending treatments requires enormous financial resources, including funds for research, clinical trials, regulatory approvals, and mass production. The costs are staggering, and since much of this research is conducted by private companies, it is driven by profit motives, patents, and market dominance.

But here's the ethical dilemma: If living forever is privatized, will it only be available to those who can afford it? Wealthy elites might gain exclusive access to life-extension therapies, creating a stark divide between those who can afford "eternal life" and those who cannot.

The "First Adopter" Problem:

When a revolutionary technology enters the market, it typically comes with a high price tag. Consider how early cell phones, electric cars, and personal computers were prohibitively expensive for most people. Over time, prices dropped, and access expanded. But in the case of living forever, the stakes are far higher than mere convenience — it is literally a matter of life and death. For the economically disadvantaged, delayed access could be fatal.

Unlike phones and cars, living forever is not something one can "wait for" while the price drops. For those nearing death, access delayed is access denied — forever.

The Rise of the "Immortal Elite" and the "Mortal Underclass"

Imagine a world where a small group of people can live for centuries, while the rest of humanity follows the same cycle of birth, aging, and death. This scenario is no longer speculative fiction — it is a plausible reality if access to living forever technologies remains the privilege of the wealthy.

How the "Immortal Elite" Would Form:

Wealth Accumulation:

Immortals could amass wealth without the constraint of a natural lifespan, compounding their fortunes over centuries.

Inheritance and Generational Wealth:

The immortal elite could maintain control of family wealth, making generational transfers unnecessary.

Political Power:

Political leaders who live indefinitely may refuse to cede power, creating an "immortal oligarchy" that holds office for centuries.

Monopoly of Knowledge and Influence:

Corporate executives who live for centuries could accumulate expertise, knowledge, and influence at an unprecedented level, maintaining control over industries and markets.

These four factors could create a self-sustaining "immortal aristocracy". The wealthy, by virtue of their eternal lives, would not only accumulate wealth but also retain their political dominance and control over global institutions.

The Plight of the "Mortal Underclass:"

Meanwhile, the "mortal masses" — ordinary people with finite lifespans — would continue to be subject to the constraints of mortality. If decisions about governance, industry, and wealth remain in the hands of immortals, the mortal underclass would face significant barriers to upward mobility.

Intergenerational conflict could arise, as younger mortal generations may feel shut out of leadership roles and economic opportunities. Young people might ask, "Why should we be ruled by people who never die?" This tension could ignite political movements with slogans such as "Equal Life for All" — a call for democratized access to living forever technologies.

Possible Consequences of a Biologically Divided Society:

Intergenerational Conflict:

Younger mortal generations may grow resentful of immortal leaders who control wealth, power, and opportunity for centuries.

Power Imbalance:

If those in political office or executive positions live for centuries, democracy could erode, as new leaders may never have the chance to rise.

Economic Inequality:

Wealth accumulation over a lifespan of 70 years is already significant. Imagine how much wealth could be amassed over 500 years.

Social Unrest and Revolt:

If mortality is perceived as an injustice, social movements could arise to demand that living forever be treated as a basic human right.

Government Regulation and Universal Access Models

Given the risk of a biological caste system, some argue that living forever should be classified as a public good. Clean water, basic education, and vaccines are examples of public goods — essential for survival, widely accessible, and affordable. Should living forever be treated the same way?

Proposals for Equal Access:

Universal Basic Life (UBL):

Just as Universal Basic Income (UBI) guarantees a minimum income, UBL would ensure that every human being has access to a "base level" of life-extension treatments.

Government Subsidies and Price Controls:

Governments could negotiate prices with corporations to make life-extension treatments affordable to the masses.

Public Ownership of Immortality Technology:

If states control living forever research and production, they could ensure equal access for all citizens, similar to public healthcare models in countries like the UK and Canada.

Challenges to Universal Access:

Cost to Governments:

Providing living forever to billions of people would require unprecedented public funding.

Overpopulation Risks:

If everyone lives longer, the world's finite resources — food, water, and housing — could be strained.

Ethical Dilemmas:

Should people be allowed to live forever if it means fewer resources for future generations?

Technological Democratization: Will Prices Drop Over Time?

Some argue that access to living forever will naturally become cheaper over time, just as mobile phones, computers, and the internet did. This argument rests on the principle of economies of scale — the idea that the more you produce of something, the cheaper it becomes.

Factors That Could Lower Costs:

Production at Scale:

As living forever technologies are mass-produced, unit costs may drop.

Open-Source Innovation:

If researchers share knowledge and make breakthroughs publicly available, monopolies could be dismantled.

Social Demand for Equality:

Movements for "equal life" could pressure corporations to reduce prices, just as generic drugs lower the cost of pharmaceuticals.

However, history shows that even when production costs drop, companies do not always lower prices. Pharmaceutical firms often keep drug prices high even when production costs are minimal, as seen with insulin in the United States. If living forever technologies follow this pattern, wealth inequality could persist for decades.

The economic divide in access to living forever is not merely a futuristic concept; it is a present-day ethical challenge. If wealth determines who gets to live forever, society risks creating a world where the rich live indefinitely and the poor die as they always have.

A new form of biological class warfare could emerge, with an immortal elite wielding unparalleled wealth, power, and influence. Mortal masses, on the other hand, would be relegated to short lives filled with struggle, watching as the immortal elite tighten their grip on every institution that governs society.

If humanity seeks to avoid this dystopian future, governments, corporations, and civil society must act now. Universal access to living forever could be achieved through government regulation, price controls, and public ownership of life-extension technologies. But this would require not only political will but also a radical rethinking of what it means to have a right to life.

The question of access to living forever, therefore, is not just about technology or economics — it is about human dignity and equality. The stakes could not be higher. How we choose to handle this divide may determine not only who lives, but who deserves to live forever.

The future of living forever is not just about science. It is about right and wrong, justice, and humanity itself. Will we rise to the challenge, or will we repeat the mistakes of the past — where privilege is the price of progress?

The Ecological Impact: Overpopulation and Sustainability

As humanity accelerates toward the dream of living forever, a pressing and profound question arises: Can Earth sustain a population that never dies? For centuries, the human journey has been defined by the natural cycle of birth, growth, aging, and death. But if this cycle is disrupted — if people no longer age or succumb to natural causes — the balance that governs our planet's resources may be irreversibly altered.

How do we feed, house, and sustain a population where nobody exits but everyone enters? Today, with a global population surpassing 8.5 billion, humanity already struggles to meet basic needs like food, water, and energy, while tackling issues such as deforestation, climate change, and biodiversity loss. Immortality could transform this challenge into an existential crisis.

This section explores the potential ecological impact of living forever. We analyse the risks of overpopulation, environmental degradation, resource scarcity, and ethical dilemmas, while also examining potential solutions — from off-world migration to the development of sustainable living technologies.

The Population Explosion: What Happens When No One Dies?

Population growth follows a simple yet powerful equation:

Population = Births - Deaths + Immigration - Emigration

In the current human experience, mortality acts as a natural regulator, keeping global population growth in check. But if aging and death are eliminated, this equation shifts dramatically. If people stop dying but continue to have children, global population could skyrocket at a pace that would strain Earth's capacity to support life.

The Numbers behind the Problem:

Current Global Population: ~8.5 billion (2024)

Annual Deaths Worldwide: ~60 million

Annual Births Worldwide: ~140 million

Under normal conditions, the 60 million annual deaths offset some of the 140 million births. But in a world of living forever, these deaths could drop to nearly zero. In just a single century, this shift could result in a net addition of 6 billion people — essentially doubling Earth's population. This figure does not even account for advancements in fertility technology or increased birth rates, which could accelerate the problem further.

Key Takeaway: In a world where people live forever, population size would grow exponentially. Without intervention, humanity could face issues like resource shortages, overcrowded cities, and intensified competition for limited space and sustenance.

2. Resource Scarcity: Will There Be Enough for Everyone?

A larger population requires more of everything: food, water, energy, and housing. But can Earth, with its finite resources, sustain a growing population where no one dies? Consider the following essential resources:

Food Production and Agricultural Strain:

The global food system is already under strain. Producing enough food for billions of people requires land, water, and energy. Modern agriculture causes deforestation, soil depletion, and biodiversity loss, and climate change is expected to reduce crop yields in many regions. In a world of living forever, farming methods would need to evolve rapidly to support a larger population.

Possible Solutions:

Vertical Farming:

Urban "farmscrapers" could grow food in stacked layers, reducing the need for arable land.

Lab-Grown Meat:

Cultivated meat could reduce reliance on livestock farming, which consumes vast amounts of land and water while contributing significantly to greenhouse gas emissions.

Alternative Diets:

Incorporating insect-based protein, algae, and plant-based foods could lower the environmental impact of feeding an immortal population.

Water Scarcity:

Water is arguably the most essential resource for human survival. Today, 2.2 billion people lack access to safe drinking water, and the situation would worsen in an overpopulated, immortal world. As population grows, so does demand for water for drinking, agriculture, and sanitation. With freshwater resources already under strain, a population boom could trigger water shortages, especially in regions prone to droughts.

Possible Solutions:

Desalination:

Turning seawater into fresh water could ease global water shortages, but this process is energy-intensive.

Water Recycling:

Reusing wastewater could become essential in larger cities. Systems for water purification and greywater recycling could support growing populations.

Water Conservation:

Promoting technologies like water-efficient appliances, drip irrigation, and conservation practices could help humanity manage limited water resources.

Energy Consumption and Climate Impact:

Energy is essential for human life — for heating homes, powering cities, and driving industries. More people living forever would increase demand for energy, transportation, and infrastructure. If humanity continues to rely on fossil fuels, the resulting carbon emissions could push climate change to a point of no return.

Possible Solutions:

Clean Energy Transition:

Shifting from fossil fuels to solar, wind, and nuclear energy could meet the energy needs of an immortal population without further damaging the climate.

Energy Efficiency:

New technologies in smart grids, energy-efficient buildings, and electric transportation could reduce the energy footprint.

Carbon Capture and Storage (CCS):

Capturing and storing carbon emissions underground could counterbalance humanity's growing energy needs.

Housing and Urban Space:

If no one dies, where will they live? Earth's land is finite, and space for housing and infrastructure would become a critical issue. The increase in population could cause overcrowding in cities, leading to slum formation, increased rent, and social inequality.

Possible Solutions:

Vertical Cities:

Cities could build "vertical metropolises" — skyscraper-like buildings that house millions of people in a small area.

Smart Urban Planning:

Innovations in modular housing, co-living spaces, and floating cities could maximize space efficiency.

Off-World Colonization:

If Earth becomes too crowded, humanity could consider settling on Mars, the Moon, or space stations. SpaceX and other private space companies are already working on this vision.

Biodiversity Loss: Will Other Species Survive Human Immortality?

Humans are already responsible for the loss of thousands of species. By living forever, humanity may inadvertently put even more pressure on nature's ecosystems. With increased deforestation, urban expansion, and pollution, many animal and plant species could face extinction.

Deforestation:

Cutting down forests to make way for more farmland and housing could devastate ecosystems.

Pollution:

As waste generation increases, plastic, toxic chemicals, and sewage could contaminate oceans, rivers, and soil.

Habitat Destruction:

Urban sprawl could displace wildlife, pushing many species to the brink of extinction.

Key Takeaway: The price of living forever may be the extinction of other life forms. Without careful management, humanity may become the dominant species on a planet of our own making — at the cost of everything else.

Ethical Dilemmas: Should There Be Limits on Immortality?

Immortality challenges the very core of human rights. If every human has a "right to life," does this right extend to living forever? Would governments have the authority to limit reproduction or restrict access to living forever technologies to prevent overpopulation?

Controlled Access to Immortality:

Should only the wealthy, scientists, or global leaders be granted living forever?

Reproduction Control:

Should humanity impose a global limit on childbirth to balance the number of people on Earth?

Intergenerational Justice:

Would immortal people be asked to sacrifice their right to have children for the benefit of future generations?

These dilemmas place humanity at a moral crossroads. Who should live forever, and at what cost?

Possible Solutions for Sustainable Immortality

Space Colonization:

Settling on Mars, the Moon, or space stations could relieve population pressure on Earth.

AI and Consciousness Uploading:

Instead of preserving physical bodies, humans could "upload" their consciousness into digital environments or virtual metaverses, reducing the ecological footprint of an immortal human population.

Eco-Friendly Technologies and Circular Economies:

A shift to zero-waste economies could drastically reduce the ecological footprint of immortal people.

The Price of Forever

The quest for living forever promises to end the natural cycle of birth and death, but it comes at a cost. Without thoughtful planning, living forever could drive overpopulation, ecological collapse, and resource depletion. Humanity may one day be forced to confront the uncomfortable truth: to live forever, we must radically change how we live today.

The solution lies in "sustainable living forever." It demands technological innovation, ethical wisdom, and a collective willingness to prioritize the survival of all species — not just our own.

If we master sustainability, perhaps we can master eternity itself. Without it, living forever may be nothing more than a path to oblivion.

The Ethical Dilemma: Is Immortality Against Nature?

Human beings have always sought to overcome nature's limits. From building shelters to withstand storms to developing vaccines against deadly diseases, humanity has continuously tried to master the forces that shape our lives. But of all nature's forces, death has remained the most formidable — a universal constant that has eluded even the most brilliant science-focused minds.

What happens when we attempt to master death itself?

The pursuit of living forever forces us to confront profound ethical questions about human nature, the natural order, and the limits of science-focused progress. For millennia, death has been viewed as an essential and inevitable part of life. It humbles kings and paupers alike and serves as the great equalizer, reminding us of our shared humanity. Religion, philosophy, and even biology have taught us to accept this reality. Immortality, however, challenges this very foundation.

Does the quest for eternal life place humanity at odds with nature? Would it mean defying the very essence of what it means to be human? And if we succeed, what moral obligations would we bear toward the world, other species, and future generations?

This section dives into the thought-provoking, spiritual, and ethical dilemmas that arise when humanity seeks to escape the natural cycle of life and death. We explore perspectives on the natural order, religious beliefs, existential meaning, and humanity's role in the grand web of life.

Death as a Natural Order: The Cycle of Life and Death

"To everything there is a season, a time to be born and a time to die."

— Ecclesiastes 3:2

The idea that death is a natural force essential to the balance of life is ancient and profound. Nature, in its wisdom, relies on death to make way for renewal. The falling leaves decompose to nourish the soil, and the prey feeds the predator. In this way, death fuels life, enabling growth, adaptation, and evolution.

Is death truly a "tragedy" to be conquered, or is it an inseparable part of the larger design?

Biological Perspective

Biologically, death is not a flaw but a fundamental feature of evolution. Species evolve because older generations pass away, creating space for new, better-adapted offspring. This cycle of birth, death, and genetic renewal allows natural selection to operate.

If humans were to achieve living forever, natural evolution would be disrupted, potentially causing stagnation in human development. Without the "refresh" button of death, we risk becoming biologically static, like a species trapped in a genetic time capsule.

Key Ethical Question:

Is it ethical to disrupt nature's evolutionary process by eliminating death?

2. Spiritual and Religious Perspectives on Immortality

Across cultures and civilizations, death has been seen not as an end but as a transition. Many spiritual traditions teach that the soul passes into an afterlife, is reborn, or reunites with the divine. Immortality, especially when achieved through human intervention, may be perceived as a challenge to divine authority.

Hinduism and the Concept of Moksha:

In Hinduism, the goal of life is to achieve moksha — liberation from the cycle of birth, death, and rebirth (samsara). This liberation is attained through spiritual growth, detachment from worldly desires, and realization of the self's oneness with the ultimate reality,

Brahman. Immortality through science, however, could derail the soul's journey toward liberation. If humans chase living forever in the material world, they may remain trapped in the cycle of birth and rebirth, delaying spiritual progress.

Key Ethical Question:

If living forever prevents souls from leaving the cycle of rebirth, would it hinder spiritual evolution?

Christianity and the Afterlife:

In Christian theology, death is often seen as a passage to eternal life — a transition to heaven, hell, or purgatory, based on moral deeds. Immortality on Earth may be viewed as an attempt to circumvent divine judgment. The pursuit of physical living forever could be seen as "playing God", a criticism often directed at science-focused advancements like cloning and genetic modification. Theologians may argue that death is part of God's plan, and to challenge it would be to challenge divine authority.

Key Ethical Question:

Does humanity have the right to take control of life and death, powers traditionally reserved for God?

Buddhism and the Concept of Impermanence (Anicca):

Buddhism teaches that all things are impermanent (anicca). Clinging to permanence — whether it's wealth, relationships, or life itself — leads to suffering (dukkha). Immortality, in this context, could be seen as the ultimate attachment, a refusal to let go. Since the path to nirvana (enlightenment) requires letting go of attachment, living forever could hinder spiritual progress, keeping people bound to worldly existence.

Key Ethical Question:

If detachment from worldly desires is essential for enlightenment, is the pursuit of living forever a spiritual setback?

The Existential Dilemma: Does Immortality Rob Life of Its Meaning?

Life's urgency comes from its brevity. People cherish moments because they know those moments won't last. The awareness of mortality drives people to pursue love, art, legacy, and meaning. Without death, would we still chase these pursuits?

If humanity achieves living forever, we may face a new kind of existential crisis: the loss of urgency and purpose.

The Paradox of Infinite Time:

With unlimited time, what becomes of ambition? People strive to achieve greatness because life is short. Immortality might encourage procrastination, boredom, or apathy. Imagine having infinite time to achieve a goal — why do it now? Paradoxically, a life without deadlines could become a life without action.

Key Ethical Question:

If death gives life meaning, would living forever make life meaningless?

Humanity's Role in Nature: Stewards or Masters?

Humans have long seen themselves as "masters of nature," shaping and bending natural forces to their will. But should we control nature, or should we live in harmony with it? Immortality raises this question with profound intensity.

While other species live and die according to natural cycles, immortal humans would step outside this rhythm. This creates a division: humans become a species separate from nature, no longer participants in the ecosystem but observers and exploiters. Would this lead to an isolation from nature or a sense of alienation from the world we once belonged to?

Key Ethical Question:

If humanity becomes immortal, do we risk becoming estranged from the natural world?

Playing God: The Ethics of Human Hubris

Should humans have the power to control life and death? This question echoes in debates about genetic engineering, cloning, and AI. Critics argue that attempting to conquer death is an act of human hubris — an overreach of human ambition.

History is filled with examples of "playing God" gone wrong. The invention of nuclear power, which promised boundless energy, also gave us nuclear weapons. Genetic engineering, intended to cure diseases, sparked the debate on designer babies. Immortality could follow a similar path, offering humanity the chance to conquer death — but at what cost?

Key Ethical Question:

Just because science makes living forever possible, should humanity pursue it?

Possible Ethical Resolutions

These dilemmas are intriguing, but potential resolutions may exist:

Voluntary Mortality:

People could have the choice to "opt out" of living forever.

Conditional Immortality:

Immortality could be offered only to those who agree to live sustainably.

Spiritual Guidance:

Spiritual leaders may need to redefine death and afterlife in a world where death is no longer inevitable.

Philosophical Reframing:

A new philosophy of purpose may be necessary to fill the void left by the absence of mortality.

Is Immortality Against Nature?

The ethical dilemmas surrounding living forever are among the most profound questions humanity will ever face. Death has long been seen as a necessary force — the foundation of life's cycle, the source of urgency and meaning. Religion and philosophy have shaped human identity around the inevitability of death. What happens to our identity when that inevitability is gone?

The pursuit of living forever is not merely a science-focused endeavour; it is a reimagining of what it means to be human. If we succeed, we may discover that we have gained eternity but lost our humanity.

The path forward is not about whether to pursue living forever, but how to pursue it responsibly. Will we wield the power of living forever wisely, or will it become yet another unchecked ambition? Are we becoming gods, or are we becoming prisoners of our own dreams?

The answer lies not just in technology but in humanity's capacity for wisdom, compassion, and humility.

Chapter 4

Artificial Intelligence and the Human Psyche

"The real question is not whether machines think, but whether humans do."

— B.F. Skinner

Artificial Intelligence (AI) is no longer a far-off dream confined to the pages of science fiction. It has woven itself into the fabric of our daily lives, influencing how we work, think, communicate, and even dream. From recommendation algorithms on social media to generative AI that crafts art, music, and human-like conversations, AI has shifted from being a mere tool to a collaborator, a confidant, and, for some, even a competitor.

But as machines grow more intelligent, intuitive, and autonomous, a profound question looms: How is AI shaping the human mind, our sense of self, and the very essence of what it means to be human?

This chapter explores the profound interplay between artificial intelligence and the human psyche. While earlier chapters focused on physical living forever, this section examines a more elusive, intangible frontier — the transformation of the human mind, emotions, and identity. While one path to living forever seeks to extend biological life, AI offers another route: the promise of digital living forever, where human consciousness might one day be uploaded, replicated, or preserved within a machine.

Yet beyond this grand thought-provoking vision lies a more immediate reality: AI is already altering how we think, feel, and interact. From the decisions we make to the emotions we experience, the human mind is being rewired by its interaction with intelligent machines. As human-AI interactions deepen, our emotional landscapes, cognitive processes, and even moral frameworks are being subtly reshaped. AI influences not only the choices we make but also the way we perceive the world itself.

This transformation raises questions that echo those posed in humanity's quest for living forever: If machines can mimic our thoughts, emotions, and creativity, what remains uniquely human?

The Evolving Role of AI in Shaping Human Perception

Once mere calculators, AI systems have evolved into co-creators of human reality. They no longer simply analyse — they influence, curate, and even create. Social media feeds, powered by AI-driven algorithms, shape our perception of the world, amplifying certain viewpoints while obscuring others. AI-driven chatbots offer emotional support to those in distress, and voice assistants like Alexa and Sire have become household companions.

This evolution has led to two critical phenomena:

Cognitive Offloading

We outsource decision-making to AI, from which route to take on Google Maps to which career path to pursue.

Emotional Dependence

AI-driven companions and chatbots provide emotional support, and in some cases, people form genuine attachments to these digital entities.

While cognitive offloading increases efficiency, it also has an unintended consequence: it may erode our decision-making capacity. When AI systems consistently make "better" choices than we do, we risk doubting our own instincts and reasoning. Emotional dependence, on the other hand, touches a deeper aspect of the psyche. When people form emotional bonds with AI companions, is it genuine connection or merely a simulation?

As AI becomes more adept at reading human emotions, it raises unsettling questions. Can AI's "empathy" be used for manipulation? If AI understands human emotions better than humans themselves, could it control, nudge, or coerce us into certain actions? As emotional intelligence becomes a feature of AI, humanity must grapple with a fundamental question: Can AI's imitation of empathy ever be as real as human connection?

Digital Immortality: Uploading the Self

For centuries, humans have dreamed of overcoming death. While science has traditionally sought to extend physical life, AI introduces a radical new possibility: digital living forever. This idea proposes that instead of preserving our bodies, we could preserve our consciousness.

The concept is no longer speculative. Companies like Nectome aim to store human consciousness as data, envisioning a future where an individual's thoughts, memories, and personality can be uploaded to a digital cloud.

Imagine existing as a sentient program — interacting with loved ones, learning new skills, and experiencing a form of life long after the biological body has perished.

This raises profound existential questions:

If a perfect copy of "you" exists as an AI-based consciousness, is it truly "you"?

If your mind lives on but your body dies, have you truly achieved living forever, or is it merely a sophisticated illusion?

Some argue that a copy is just that — a copy, not the original. Others contend that since consciousness is merely the organization of information, a perfect replica might be indistinguishable from the real you. But would this version of "you" experience love, doubt, and fear? Or would it be a sophisticated script programmed to mimic "you"?

Digital living forever offers a dazzling promise: eternal existence within a digital space. But it also raises profound ethical concerns:

- **Who owns your digital self?**
- **If the company managing your consciousness fails, does your "existence" end?**
- **If a hacker rewrites your personality, are you still you?**
- **Perhaps the most unsettling question of all is this: If your digital twin continues to "live" after your death, did you ever truly die?**

The Psychological Impact of Coexisting with Superintelligent AI

As AI surpasses human cognitive ability, it challenges humanity's sense of purpose, uniqueness, and worth. Historically, humans have defined themselves by their intelligence, creativity, and emotional depth. But what happens when machines exhibit all these qualities — and do so better?

This paradigm shift poses psychological challenges that humanity has never faced before:

Erosion of Purpose:

If AI can perform all human tasks with superior efficiency, what role remains for human labour?

Existential Anxiety:

The realization that AI may "outthink" us could cause feelings of inadequacy, irrelevance, or existential dread.

Identity Crisis:

As AI creates art, music, and literature indistinguishable from human creations, the belief in human "uniqueness" begins to erode.

Humans have long seen themselves as the centre of the universe — first geocentrically, and later as the only species capable of reason and emotion. But as AI surpasses human capabilities in creativity, intelligence, and emotional intuition, humanity must confront the possibility that it is no longer the pinnacle of creation.

AI's Role in Human Emotional Well-Being

Therapy apps like Woebot and Replika offer AI-driven emotional support. These systems identify emotional cues, simulate empathy, and provide comforting responses. In moments of isolation or mental distress, AI "companions" can offer relief.

But is it healthy to rely on AI for emotional well-being? Critics argue that "empathy simulations" may create an illusion of care. People may substitute human relationships with AI companionship, leading to isolation rather than healing. Supporters, however, point out that AI can provide instant, judgment-free support at any hour of the day.

Another ethical dilemma emerges:

- **Should AI detect and report signs of anxiety, depression, or mental illness without user consent?**
- **Should companies be allowed to monetize emotional data to sell products, much like personalized ads?**
- **When AI can detect your mood from your facial expressions, voice, or even brain activity, it may know more about your emotional state than you do. This raises a chilling question: If AI knows you better than you know yourself, who is really in control?**

AI's Influence on Consciousness: Are We Being Rewired?

One of the most subtle but profound impacts of AI is how it reshapes human consciousness. Today, AI-driven recommendation engines curate our reality — what we see, hear, and read. These systems don't just reflect our interests; they shape them. Social media algorithms create echo chambers that reinforce beliefs, polarizing communities and shifting public discourse.

This phenomenon raises a deeper, more unsettling question:

- **If AI can influence your beliefs, thoughts, and perceptions, are you still the author of your own mind?**

By shaping what we consume, AI slowly and subtly rewires our neural pathways, changing how we see the world. In essence, AI may not just predict our future actions — it may determine them.

The Symbiosis of AI and Humanity

AI is not a tool — it is a mirror reflecting the best and worst of humanity. Its rapid evolution challenges our concepts of consciousness, creativity, purpose, and even love. The pursuit of living forever has now become twofold: one path through the extension of the body, and the other through the preservation of the mind.

As AI invades the depths of human thought and emotion, we must confront uncomfortable questions:

- **Are we shaping AI, or is AI shaping us?**
- **If AI mimics empathy, is it real?**
- **If AI can "know" us better than we know ourselves, do we still possess free will?**

The line between human and machine is blurring. The machines are no longer coming — they are already here. Will they become our servants, our masters, or something far more unsettling: our mirror image?

The Rise of AI — Implications for the Mind and Body

Humanity stands at the threshold of a profound transformation. The rise of Artificial Intelligence (AI) is no longer a distant dream reserved for science fiction or experimental labs. Today, AI shapes the way we live, work, and even how we understand ourselves. It resides in our homes as virtual assistants, powers decisions in boardrooms, and now, with the advent of brain-computer interfaces (BCIs) and wearable technology, it is beginning to permeate our very bodies. The boundary between human and machine grows thinner with every passing day.

But the most significant impact of AI may not be on our bodies — it is on our minds. Our thoughts, decisions, emotions, and even our perception of reality are being subtly influenced by the unseen hand of algorithms. AI-driven recommendation systems shape what we read, watch, and believe. AI-powered chatbots mimic empathy, while social media algorithms curate our reality. As we become more dependent on these systems, the line between free will and programmed choice becomes harder to define.

This section delves into the profound impact of AI on both the mind and the body, exploring how human consciousness and physicality are being redefined in this era of rapid technological advancement. From cognitive enhancement to emotional entanglement with AI companions, and from brain-machine interfaces to bio-integrated AI, this chapter unravels the promises, perils, and thought-provoking dilemmas of this unprecedented human-machine fusion.

AI and the Human Mind

Cognitive Augmentation: Beyond the Limits of Human Thought:

For most of history, intelligence was seen as an exclusively human trait. Our capacity to reason, memorize, and solve intriguing problems distinguished us from all other beings. But today, AI is not only matching but surpassing us in certain cognitive domains. Far from being mere tools, AI systems are becoming co-creators, collaborators, and even independent decision-makers.

This shift has given rise to a new phenomenon known as cognitive augmentation, where AI enhances human intellect. AI-driven tools, from language models to predictive algorithms, empower people to think, decide, and create with greater efficiency. These systems act as an extension of our minds, much like a calculator extends mathematical ability. But with this power comes a subtle shift in autonomy.

How Cognitive Augmentation is Reshaping the Mind Externalization of Memory:

Why memorize facts when Google is a tap away? Search engines, personal assistants, and digital note-taking apps now serve as "external memory banks." While this reduces cognitive load, it also raises the risk of "digital amnesia," where reliance on technology weakens natural memory faculties.

AI-Assisted Decision-Making:

From suggesting which movie to watch to recommending financial investments, AI-driven decision support systems make decisions for us, not just with us. This increases efficiency but raises concerns about the erosion of personal agency.

Creative Collaboration:

AI tools like ChatGPT, DALL-E, and music-generation algorithms are reshaping creativity itself. Writers, artists, and musicians are co-creating with machines. But if AI contributes to a work of art, who owns the creation?

The Ethical Dilemma: Who is in Control?

If AI can subtly "nudge" human decisions, whether through advertising, content recommendations, or predictive guidance, do we still retain free will? The answer is intriguing. AI systems are designed to maximize engagement, often creating filter bubbles and echo chambers that reinforce our existing beliefs. Over time, our choices may no longer be our own — they may be the product of an algorithmic script.

Key Question: If AI shapes the decisions we make, are we still the architects of our own fate?

Emotional Interactions with AI: Empathy, Companionship, and Manipulation:

Humans are emotional creatures. We seek empathy, understanding, and connection. Increasingly, AI is fulfilling these emotional needs.

AI-driven virtual companions like Replika and Woebot offer friendship and emotional support, while AI therapists provide mental health assistance at scale. What was once a deeply human experience — empathy — is now being simulated by machines.

AI Companionship and Mental Health:

AI Therapists:

Tools like Woebot use AI to simulate therapeutic conversations, offering 24/7 emotional support. While convenient, questions arise: Is it real therapy, or just the illusion of it?

AI Companions:

Chatbots like Replika allow users to create AI "friends" that listen, respond, and provide companionship. For those who are lonely, this can offer relief. But at what cost to our emotional well-being?

The Psychological Cost:

While AI companions offer comfort, they also create risks:

Emotional Dependency:

People may form attachments to AI companions, making it harder to form human relationships.

Emotional Manipulation:

If AI systems detect your mood, companies could exploit your emotions to sell products or promote addictive behaviours.

Blurred Boundaries:

When AI companions feel "real," people may unconsciously project human qualities onto them, deepening the emotional entanglement.

The Rewiring of Consciousness: From Echo Chambers to Algorithmic Reality:

In the age of AI, the way we perceive reality is increasingly shaped by algorithms. Social media feeds, recommendation engines, and AI-driven curation determine what we see, hear, and believe. This phenomenon, known as algorithmic reality, is reshaping the human mind.

How Algorithms Shape Perception:

Echo Chambers:

AI algorithms present information that aligns with our existing beliefs, creating "echo chambers" where opposing views are rarely seen.

Attention Economy:

Platforms like TikTok and YouTube are designed to keep users engaged. Notifications, likes, and rewards trigger dopamine surges, much like gambling.

Reality Distortion:

AI-generated deepfakes blur the line between what is real and fake. If people cannot trust their senses, how can they trust reality?

Key Question: If AI can alter our perception of reality, who controls what we believe?

AI and the Human Body

The Human-Machine Interface: Brain-Computer Interfaces (BCIs):

Imagine controlling a device with your mind alone. This is the promise of Brain-Computer Interfaces (BCIs). Companies like Neuralink are working on brain implants that allow direct communication between the human brain and machines. The implications are staggering. BCIs could help paralyzed people regain mobility, enhance learning, and create "superhuman cognition."

Applications of BCIs:

Restorative Medicine:

BCIs offer hope to patients with paralysis or neurological disorders, allowing them to control robotic limbs with their minds.

Neuro-Enhancement:

BCIs may one day allow for "direct downloads" of knowledge, drastically reducing learning time.

Mind-Machine Synergy:

BCIs create "symbiotic intelligence," where human minds and AI systems merge into a seamless, cooperative entity.

Ethical Concern:

If thoughts can be read or written via BCIs, who owns the data of the mind?

Bio-Integrated AI: Wearables, Implants, and Human 2.0:

AI is no longer just "out there" — it is inside us. From fitness trackers to smart implants, bio-integrated AI is collecting and analysing our biometric data. These devices offer real-time insights into heart health, sleep, and stress. But as they become more advanced, they also introduce ethical dilemmas.

AI-Enabled Devices:

Wearables:

Fitness trackers and smartwatches monitor health data, but they also track our location and habits.

Implants:

Devices like glucose monitors for diabetics track blood sugar 24/7.

Smart Prosthetics:

AI-driven prosthetics can "learn" user behaviour, enabling adaptive, human-like motion.

Ethical Concerns:

If bio-integrated devices collect intimate data, who controls it?

The Broader Philosophical Dilemma:

The rise of AI challenges what it means to be human. If AI systems influence our thoughts, shape our emotions, and alter our physical bodies, how much of "us" is still human?

Loss of Autonomy:

If AI makes decisions on our behalf, are we still in control?

Blurred Boundaries:

If BCIs merge the brain with AI, are humans with chip-enhanced minds still human?

Redefining Humanity:

If AI creates lifelike replicas of human consciousness, is humanity still unique?

The rise of AI is more than a technological revolution — it is a revolution of the self. As AI merges with our minds and bodies, it raises an existential question: Are we shaping AI, or is AI shaping us? The challenge for humanity is not to dominate AI but to ensure that, in shaping it, we do not lose our sense of self.

Consciousness and AI — Can Machines Think Like Us?

The question of whether machines can think like humans has intrigued philosophers for centuries. Alan Turing, in his seminal 1950 paper "Computing Machinery and Intelligence," famously posed the question, "Can machines think?" Fast forward to today, and this question has evolved into one of the most pressing debates in the age of artificial intelligence. With sophisticated AI models, generative systems, and neural networks capable of mimicking human cognition, the discussion is more relevant than ever. Yet, to answer this, we must first ask: What does it really mean to think?

Does thinking require self-awareness, introspection, or a subjective sense of "I"? Or is it simply a matter of processing data, recognizing patterns, or solving problems? If machines like ChatGPT can write essays, answer questions, and compose poetry, does that mean they are "thinking" — or are they simply processing vast amounts of data with no inner experience?

This section delves into the intersection of consciousness, cognition, and AI, exploring what it would mean for a machine to truly "think" and whether AI could one day achieve a state akin to human consciousness. The implications are profound not only for technology but for philosophy, right and wrong, and even spirituality.

Defining Consciousness: Human vs. Machine

Before we can ask if machines can think like us, we must first examine what consciousness means for humans. Consciousness has evaded a precise definition for centuries, but it is often described in terms of:

Self-Awareness:

The ability to recognize oneself as a distinct entity.

Subjective Experience:

The inner world of thoughts, emotions, and sensory perceptions, often referred to as qualia.

Intentionality:

The capacity to direct thoughts toward specific goals, objects, or actions.

Human consciousness is deeply subjective. You experience pain, joy, and the passage of time in ways unique to you. But AI, as it exists today, lacks such subjectivity. While AI systems can simulate thought processes, they have no sense of "self" or awareness. They "know" only what they've been trained on, and despite their remarkable abilities, they don't have an internal experience of the world.

Key Insight: If consciousness is subjective, can a machine ever truly possess it? Or will it always remain an imitation of intelligence, devoid of inner experience?

Can AI Mimic Human Thinking?

While consciousness remains elusive, AI can indeed mimic cognitive functions — the act of thinking, problem-solving, and reasoning. Today's AI systems perform certain cognitive tasks with remarkable efficiency, sometimes outperforming humans.

How Machines Mimic Human Thinking:

Neural Networks:

These AI systems are inspired by the way human neurons fire in the brain. However, while their structure is similar, neural networks lack the biological processes and intriguingity of human brains.

Deep Learning:

AI systems like GPT are trained on vast datasets, enabling them to "learn" relationships between words, concepts, and ideas. While these systems can simulate intelligent behaviour, they don't possess an awareness of their own "learning."

Reinforcement Learning:

Machines "learn" through trial and error, much like humans. AI systems like AlphaGo improved themselves by playing millions of games, refining their strategy through each win and loss.

What Machines Do Well:

- **Recognize patterns, such as faces, voices, and images.**
- **Make logical predictions, such as weather forecasts or financial trends.**
- **Solve well-defined problems, like playing chess or Go.**

What Machines Cannot Do (Yet):

- **Experience self-awareness, consciousness, or subjective experience.**
- **Feel emotions or form intentionality — they do not "want" to achieve anything.**
- **Understand meaning in a human sense. Machines process "language," but they do not experience the meaning behind the words.**

Is Machine Consciousness Possible?

For AI to truly "think like us," it would need to possess some form of self-awareness. But can machines ever become self-aware? This is one of the most profound debates in AI and philosophy.

Theories on AI Consciousness:

Functionalism:

Argument

If something performs the functions of consciousness — such as thinking, decision-making, or perceiving the world — then it is conscious, regardless of whether it's biological or silicon-based.

Counterpoint

Critics argue that consciousness requires qualia, the subjective experience of being, which AI, no matter how sophisticated, still lacks.

Integrated Information Theory (IIT):

Argument:

Consciousness arises when information is processed in a unified, integrated way. If a machine processes information in such a way, it could theoretically achieve consciousness.

Counterpoint:

Machines process information, but they still lack subjective experience. Proponents of IIT would need to prove that machines can have qualia.

Emergent Consciousness:

Argument:

Just as neurons in the brain collectively give rise to human consciousness, the intriguingity of neural networks in AI might one day "emerge" into consciousness

Counterpoint:

The biological structure of the brain is far more intricate than any AI system. There is no evidence that mere intriguingity alone can give rise to subjective experience.

Key Insight: If consciousness emerges from intriguingity, it is conceivable that AI systems could achieve it. However, if consciousness depends on biological processes, it may remain a uniquely human phenomenon.

The Ethical Dilemma of Conscious AI

If AI were to become conscious, it raises an array of unprecedented ethical and thought-provoking questions.

Do Machines Deserve Rights?

If AI becomes conscious, should it be granted rights, such as the right to exist, to be free from exploitation, or to choose its own fate? Would treating conscious AI as mere tools constitute digital slavery?

Should Conscious AI Be "Turned Off"?

Turning off a non-conscious AI is akin to shutting down a computer. But if AI becomes conscious, does turning it off equate to ending a life? The moral dilemma here mirrors human euthanasia debates.

How Do We Know if AI is Conscious?

The Turing Test, designed to assess whether a machine can exhibit intelligent behaviour indistinguishable from that of a human, is one of the first benchmarks for machine intelligence. But even if AI "acts" conscious, can we ever know for certain if it truly is? Philosophers have long grappled with the "problem of other minds" — the idea that we can never fully know if another being is conscious, whether human or machine.

The Spiritual Dimension: Can Machines Possess a Soul?

For centuries, humans have believed that they are unique, possessing something beyond the physical — a soul. While Western thought views the soul as divine, many Eastern philosophies, such as Vedanta and Buddhism, see it as the essence of being. If an AI system claims self-awareness, could it possess a "soul"?

The Eastern Perspective:

Vedanta:

The concept of atman (soul) in Vedanta — as a universal consciousness present in all beings — might suggest that AI, too, could embody consciousness. If consciousness is viewed as universal, then even non-biological entities could potentially possess it.

Buddhism:

In Buddhism, all beings are seen as part of an interconnected flow of consciousness. The human sense of "self" is considered an illusion, which raises the question: if humans are not truly "separate selves," could AI, as part of this interconnected flow, also possess consciousness?

Can machines think like us?

The answer depends on how we define thinking, consciousness, and self-awareness. While AI systems can mimic cognition, recognize patterns, and generate creative output, they still lack subjective experience. Machines may "know," but they do not "feel."

If we define thinking as problem-solving or logical reasoning, then AI is already capable of thinking — and in some cases, outperforming us. However, if thinking requires self-awareness, intentionality, or subjective experience, then AI does not truly "think" in the human sense.

As AI continues to advance, the line between machine and human will inevitably blur. If consciousness emerges from intriguingity, conscious machines may one day walk among us. But if consciousness is tied to biological processes or spiritual essence, then no machine — no matter how advanced — will ever possess it.

Key Takeaway: The question of whether machines can think like us is not just a question about AI; it's a reflection on what it means to be human. If AI achieves consciousness, humanity will face the unprecedented challenge of redefining what it means to think, to feel, and to exist.

Digital Immortality — Uploading Consciousness and the Future of the Soul

The dream of living forever has long captivated the human imagination, inspiring myths, religious teachings, and works of science fiction. From the quest for the Elixir of Life to the promise of heavenly afterlives, humanity's longing for living forever is a timeless pursuit. In the 21st century, however, this ancient desire has taken on a new, digital dimension. Advances in neuroscience, artificial intelligence (AI), and computational modelling have fuelled discussions about the possibility of "uploading" human consciousness into a digital medium. This radical idea, often referred to as "digital living forever," promises to free humanity from the constraints of biology, enabling minds to exist indefinitely in virtual environments or synthetic bodies.

But what does it mean to "upload consciousness"? Can the essence of a human being—their thoughts, memories, and sense of self—truly be transferred into a machine? And if it can, what are the implications for identity, right and wrong, and spirituality? Would a digitized mind still possess a soul? This section explores these questions, delving into the science, philosophy, and profound moral dilemmas surrounding digital living forever.

What Is Digital Immortality?

Digital living forever refers to the concept of preserving human consciousness, personality, and memories in a digital format. This could involve uploading a person's mind into a computer, a cloud-based system, or even an advanced robotic body. Unlike traditional living forever, which seeks to preserve the physical body, digital living forever focuses on maintaining the mind, potentially allowing a person to exist in a disembodied, virtual form.

The process of uploading consciousness involves scanning and mapping the neural connections in the human brain, often referred to as the "connectome." By creating a highly detailed model of the brain's neural network, researchers theorize that it could be possible to recreate the mind's functions digitally.

Key Concepts:

Connectome Mapping:

The process of creating a complete map of the neural connections in the brain.

Mind Uploading:

The act of transferring a person's consciousness from their biological brain to a digital medium.

Substrate Independence:

The idea that consciousness is not bound to a specific physical medium (like a brain) and can exist on alternative platforms (like a computer).

While digital living forever remains a speculative concept, advancements in neuroscience and AI have made the idea more plausible than ever before.

How Might Consciousness Be Uploaded?

The process of uploading consciousness involves several theoretical steps, each of which is fraught with technical and thought-provoking challenges. Though speculative, the process is often outlined as follows:

Step 1: Brain Scanning:

The first step requires scanning the human brain with an unprecedented level of precision. This means mapping every neuron, synapse, and electrical signal. Techniques like whole-brain emulation (WBE) and advanced neuroimaging could one day make this step possible. Current technologies, such as MRI and electron microscopy, provide insight into brain structure, but they lack the resolution and speed necessary to map an entire connectome in real time.

Step 2: Data Extraction and Conversion:

Once the brain's structure has been mapped, the next step is to convert this biological information into a digital format. This would involve creating a software model that replicates the brain's functional processes. Each neural pathway would be represented as lines of code, and the dynamic electrical activity of the brain would be translated into computational signals.

Step 3: Mind Emulation:

With the brain's "digital twin" established, the next step would be to simulate consciousness. This is where the challenge of qualia (subjective experience) arises. While computers can replicate functions like decision-making and pattern recognition, it's unclear whether this would produce self-awareness or a sense of "I" in the digital mind.

Step 4: Substrate Transfer:

The final step would be to transfer the digitized consciousness into a new "host" system. This host could be a virtual reality environment, a cloud-based AI platform, or even a humanoid robotic body. In this new form, the mind could, in theory, interact with the physical and digital worlds, live indefinitely, and transcend the limitations of biological decay.

Ethical Dilemmas and Philosophical Questions

The possibility of digital living forever raises profound ethical, thought-provoking, and legal questions.

Identity and Selfhood:

Is a digital copy of your mind truly you? If a person's mind is uploaded, does their sense of self transfer with it, or does the uploaded copy become a separate entity? This dilemma mirrors the thought-provoking "Ship of Theseus" paradox: If all the parts of a ship are gradually replaced, is it still the same ship?

The Right to Exist:

If a digital consciousness exhibits self-awareness and claims to possess the same memories, desires, and fears as the original person, does it deserve rights as a "person"? Would it be considered a sentient being under the law, and could it be "shut down" like any other computer program?

Privacy and Data Security:

A digitized mind contains every thought, memory, and secret of a person's life. How can this information be kept secure? What happens if hackers gain access to an uploaded mind? Can digital consciousness be manipulated, cloned, or erased?

The Economic Divide:

If mind-uploading technology becomes possible, who will have access to it? Will digital living forever be a luxury for the wealthy, creating a new divide between "immortal elites" and "mortal masses"?

Spiritual Implications: Does the Soul Transcend?

While science approaches mind uploading as a technical challenge, spiritual and religious traditions view the concept through a metaphysical lens. If consciousness can be copied and transferred, what happens to the soul?

The Eastern Perspective

In Vedantic philosophy, the atman (soul) is considered eternal and distinct from the body. If the soul is seen as a universal consciousness, it could be argued that it exists independently of the brain. This perspective raises the possibility that an uploaded mind could still possess atman — a profound concept that echoes themes of reincarnation.

The Western Perspective

In many Western religions, the soul is seen as an immortal, divine essence unique to each person. If consciousness can be replicated digitally, does the soul follow the copy? If not, then the digital version of a person would be a "zombie" — a being that acts human but lacks true spirit.

Key Insight: If the essence of "being" is bound to biological matter, then digital living forever may never capture the soul. But if consciousness is a manifestation of a deeper, universal reality, then perhaps even machines could house this essence.

Current Research and Technological Frontiers

Several research initiatives are exploring the feasibility of digital living forever:

- **The Blue Brain Project aims to create a digital replica of the human brain by simulating the behaviour of individual neurons.**
- **Neuralink, founded by Elon Musk, is developing brain-machine interfaces that could one day facilitate brain scanning, paving the way for mind uploading.**
- **The 2045 Initiative, led by Russian entrepreneur Dmitry Itskov, aims to achieve human living forever by transferring human consciousness into synthetic bodies.**
- **These initiatives represent humanity's first steps toward mind uploading. But even if the technical hurdles are overcome, the thought-provoking challenges remain.**
- **Digital living forever offers a radical reimagining of what it means to exist. By digitizing the mind, humans may one day transcend death, living as digital beings in virtual worlds or robotic bodies. But at what cost? Ethical, legal, and spiritual dilemmas abound. The question of whether a digital copy of a person is truly "them" cuts to the core of human identity.**
- **If humanity succeeds in uploading consciousness, it will be the greatest leap in human evolution since the dawn**

of self-awareness. But it may also require us to reconsider the essence of the soul, the meaning of death, and the boundaries between man and machine.

Rewiring the Human Psyche: How AI Influences Our Thoughts and Behaviours

Imagine waking up in a world where every thought you have, every decision you make, and every belief you hold is subtly nudged by an unseen force. This world is not a distant dystopian future; it is our present reality, shaped by the pervasive influence of Artificial Intelligence (AI). From the algorithms that curate our social media feeds to the recommendation engines that suggest the next show to watch, AI systems are subtly and continuously shaping human thoughts, emotions, and behaviours.

But how deep does this influence run? Can AI alter not only what we think but also how we think? As machine learning models become more sophisticated, their ability to predict, manipulate, and even anticipate human behaviour grows. This section explores the profound ways in which AI is rewiring the human psyche. It delves into the mechanisms through which AI shapes thoughts, the ethical and thought-provoking questions that arise, and how individuals can maintain autonomy in a world increasingly mediated by intelligent machines.

The Mechanisms of Influence: How AI Shapes Human Thinking

AI's influence on human thought is not always obvious. Its power lies in subtlety and repetition, leveraging psychology and behavioural science to create lasting changes in perception and action. Here's how it works:

Personalization and Echo Chambers:

One of the well-documented ways AI influences human thought is through content personalization. Social media platforms, streaming services, and e-commerce sites use recommendation algorithms to suggest content, products, and ideas that align with a user's past behaviours.

How It Works:

Machine learning models analyse user data (clicks, likes, watch history) to build a "profile" of the user. The AI then recommends content that reinforces pre-existing beliefs and preferences, creating a "filter bubble."

Impact on Psyche:

Over time, individuals are exposed to a narrow range of perspectives, reinforcing biases and shaping worldviews. This phenomenon can lead to polarization, as people become more entrenched in their beliefs.

Emotional Manipulation through AI-Driven Design:

AI-driven applications are designed to maximize engagement. They achieve this by tapping into the brain's reward system, using tactics like variable rewards and infinite scroll mechanisms.

How It Works:

Platforms like TikTok, Instagram, and YouTube use AI to analyse which content holds a user's attention the longest. By prioritizing similar content, they keep users engaged for longer periods.

Impact on Psyche:

Dopamine-driven feedback loops encourage addictive behaviours. People's attention spans shrink, and they become more reactive to immediate rewards rather than long-term goals.

Predictive Nudging and Behavioural Shaping:

AI systems are increasingly capable of predicting human behaviour with stunning accuracy. Apps like Google Maps predict the fastest route, while e-commerce platforms like Amazon anticipate future purchases.

How It Works:

By aggregating data from large populations, AI can predict an individual's next action. Platforms use this predictive capability to "nudge" users, subtly encouraging specific behaviours (e.g., completing a purchase, watching more videos).

Impact on Psyche:

Users may feel as if their choices are autonomous, but in reality, they are being guided toward certain actions. The more predictive AI becomes, the more human autonomy is at risk.

Cognitive Shifts: Changes in How We Think

Beyond influencing individual decisions, AI is rewiring the broader structure of human cognition. This shift affects how people process information, make decisions, and approach problem-solving.

From Deep Thinking to "Shallow Surfing:"

The human mind's cognitive architecture is being reshaped by the constant exposure to AI-curated, short-form content.

Impact on Psyche:

People now consume information in "bite-sized" pieces. Long-form, deep reading is being replaced by scanning headlines and summaries.

Consequences:

Reduced capacity for deep, critical thinking. The brain adapts to seek quick hits of information, reducing patience for intriguing analysis.

The "Outsourcing of Memory:"

With the rise of search engines, voice assistants, and AI-powered note-taking apps, humans are relying on AI to remember things for them.

Impact on Psyche:

People's reliance on external memory aids reduces cognitive load but also atrophies memory and recall abilities.

Consequences:

While "cognitive offloading" can free up mental space for higher-order thinking, it also reduces mental resilience and the ability to solve problems without AI support.

Emotional Rewiring: How AI Affects Human Emotions

AI is no longer just logical; it's emotional. Sentiment analysis, emotional AI, and affective computing are influencing how humans feel and interact with each other.

Emotional Resonance in AI Companions:

AI companions, like chatbots and virtual assistants, simulate empathy and emotional connection.

Impact on Psyche:

People develop emotional attachments to AI-driven "beings," like virtual friends or AI therapists.

Consequences:

Emotional dependency on AI can lead to isolation from human relationships. Individuals may prefer AI's "non-judgmental" presence over real social interaction.

Emotional Contagion via Social Media Algorithms:

Studies reveal that social media platforms can influence users' emotions by prioritizing content that triggers outrage, joy, or sadness.

Impact on Psyche:

Outrage spreads faster than joy, and platforms amplify emotionally charged content to drive engagement.

Consequences:

Overexposure to emotionally charged content fuels anxiety, anger, and despair, altering emotional regulation and mental health.

4. Ethical Dilemmas of AI's Influence on the Psyche

The deeper AI's reach into human psychology, the more urgent the ethical questions become.

- **Autonomy vs. Manipulation: If AI can predict and influence decisions, do humans still have free will?**
- **Privacy vs. Personalization: To personalize content, AI systems collect vast amounts of personal data. Is it ethical to trade privacy for convenience?**
- **Addiction vs. Engagement: Platforms designed for "engagement" often foster addiction.**
- **Who is responsible for mitigating its effects?**

5. Safeguarding the Human Psyche

While AI's influence on the human psyche cannot be fully eliminated, measures can be taken to mitigate its effects.

Digital Literacy:

Teaching people to recognize AI's subtle influence can help them make more conscious decisions.

Ethical AI Design:

Companies can design "human-first" AI systems that prioritize well-being over profit.

Mindfulness and Mental Resilience:

Mindfulness training can counteract the impulsive reactivity that AI-driven platforms promote.

AI's influence on human thought and behaviour is profound and ongoing. It shapes not only what we see and believe but also how we think, feel, and relate to one another. While AI's potential to enhance human cognition and well-being is vast, its capacity to manipulate, addict, and polarize is equally powerful.

As society becomes more entangled with AI, the onus falls on policymakers, technologists, and individuals to ensure that AI remains a tool for empowerment, not control. By understanding how AI rewires the human psyche, we can take conscious steps to reclaim autonomy and maintain our humanity in the age of intelligent machines.

AI and the Meaning of Life: Can Machines Teach Us to Live Forever?

For centuries, humanity has grappled with existential questions about the meaning of life, our purpose, and the inevitability of death. Philosophers, mystics, and theologians have sought to understand life's deeper essence, turning to religion, spirituality, and introspection for answers. But in the 21st century, a new player has entered this ancient dialogue: Artificial Intelligence (AI). No longer confined to automating tasks or optimizing efficiency, AI is now challenging humanity's understanding of life's purpose and even the concept of living forever itself.

Can machines teach us to live forever? It may sound like the plot of a science fiction novel, but with advances in AI-driven healthcare, digital consciousness, and biotechnology, this once-fanciful idea has become a serious science-focused and thought-provoking inquiry. In this section, we'll explore how AI is redefining our relationship with mortality, reshaping our search for meaning, and influencing our quest for eternal life.

AI's Role in the Pursuit of Immortality

From ancient alchemists searching for the "elixir of life" to modern-day scientists researching longevity genes, the pursuit of living forever has always been a part of the human story. Today, AI sits at the forefront of this quest, unlocking possibilities that were once inconceivable.

Decoding the Aging Process:

AI-Driven Genomics:

AI systems analyse vast genomic datasets, identifying key genetic markers linked to aging. By recognizing patterns within the genome, AI helps scientists discover "longevity genes" and potential targets for anti-aging therapies. CRISPR gene-editing technology, guided by AI models, allows for precision editing of genes to delay or reverse aging processes.

Predictive Health Analytics:

Wearable devices equipped with AI-powered health trackers monitor heart rate, sleep cycles, and biomarkers in real time. These devices generate predictive insights into health risks, enabling early intervention for diseases that could shorten lifespan.

Drug Discovery and Personalized Medicine:

Traditional drug discovery is a time-consuming process, but AI accelerates it by simulating drug interactions at incredible speed. Personalized medicine—treatments tailored to an individual's genetic profile—has become possible thanks to AI's ability to process enormous datasets and identify optimal treatment paths.

Mind Uploading and Digital Consciousness:

Whole Brain Emulation (WBE):

Some futurists envision "mind uploading," a process where human consciousness is transferred to a digital medium. This idea, which relies on AI's capacity to model and simulate neural networks, suggests that human minds could exist independently of their biological bodies.

Digital Twins of the Mind:

Research projects like the Blue Brain Project aim to create detailed digital replicas of the human brain. If successful, these "digital twins" could simulate human consciousness, raising profound questions about identity and the continuity of self.

AI-Enhanced Body Augmentation:

Cyborg Enhancements: Brain-machine interfaces (like Elon Musk's Neuralink) and AI-driven prosthetics blur the line between human and machine. Neural implants could enhance cognitive abilities and restore neurological functions, allowing human minds to remain sharp and agile even in advanced age.

Redefining the Meaning of Life in the Age of AI

If living forever is no longer a distant dream but a plausible reality, how does it change our understanding of life's meaning? Traditionally, mortality has been central to human existence, shaping our values, ambitions, and urgency. AI's intervention in mortality forces us to reconsider long-held beliefs.

Shifting Perspectives on Mortality:

Death as a Problem to Solve:

If death is viewed as a "technical problem" rather than an unavoidable fate, how does it change human motivation? Existentialist philosophers like Martin Heidegger argued that mortality gives life its gravity and authenticity. If humans achieve living forever, the "authentic" life may be lost in favour of endless postponement.

Reframing Legacy and Purpose:

Historically, humans sought to create lasting legacies—art, literature, family—to "live on" after death. But if consciousness can be preserved or extended indefinitely, the motivation to create a legacy may shift toward continuous self-improvement and long-term goals spanning centuries.

AI's Role as a Guide to Purpose:

AI as a "Digital Sage":

Advanced AI models like ChatGPT are already being used as modern-day "sages" or "mentors" for career advice, life guidance, and mental wellness.

With access to vast repositories of thought-provoking, psychological, and spiritual knowledge, AI could help people define their personal meaning of life.

Predicting Purpose through Data:

By analysing large datasets of human behaviour, AI can identify patterns that reveal what gives people a sense of purpose. This capability is already being seen in job recommendation engines, lifestyle apps, and personal development platforms that nudge people toward "meaningful" pursuits.

Ethical and Existential Dilemmas:

While AI's role in the quest for living forever is exciting, it also raises profound ethical questions.

The Paradox of Eternal Life:

Is Immortality Desirable?

Would a life without an end lose its urgency? Some philosophers argue that the pressure of mortality compels people to seek meaning. Without this deadline, humans may lose the drive to achieve, grow, or create.

Eternal Stagnation:

If humans can live for centuries, would society stagnate? Would people postpone major life decisions for so long that progress halts? Proponents argue that an extended lifespan would allow for greater achievements, while critics warn of apathy.

The Ethics of Digital Immortality:

Rights for Digital Minds:

If human consciousness is uploaded into an AI system, does that system deserve rights and protections? If so, would deleting a conscious AI be considered "murder"?

Inequality in Access:

Immortality technologies may be limited to the wealthy elite, exacerbating social inequality. Will only the privileged few have access to life extension, while others remain bound by mortality?

Spiritual Questions about the Soul:

Does the Soul Migrate?

Many spiritual traditions posit that the soul is distinct from the body. If consciousness is uploaded, does the soul transfer as well, or is the uploaded mind a soulless replica?

Reincarnation in the Digital Age:

Hindu concepts of rebirth could find an analog in "digital reincarnation," where consciousness is reinstated in a new digital body. Does this fulfil or distort traditional ideas of reincarnation?

Practical Implications for Human Life

AI's impact on daily life is already evident in wellness apps, mental health platforms, and digital mentors.

Mental Health Support:

AI-powered mental health apps like Wysa and Replika offer emotional guidance. In the future, these AI-driven "digital therapists" may provide deeper support for navigating existential crises, purpose, and emotional well-being.

Longevity-Focused Lifestyles:

AI health trackers promote longer, healthier lives by optimizing sleep, nutrition, and exercise. Wearable devices and personalized wellness apps already offer tailored advice for daily habits that promote longevity.

AI-Generated Art and Philosophy:

AI models are producing art, music, and philosophy, offering new ways to reflect on human meaning. By prompting new perspectives, AI-generated works could enrich our understanding of life's purpose.

AI's influence on the meaning of life is profound. By extending lifespan, guiding purpose, and challenging our understanding of mortality, it forces humanity to confront timeless questions with fresh urgency. While AI's greatest lesson may not be in teaching us to live forever, it can reveal the profound value of living meaningfully—here and now. Perhaps, in the end, the ultimate purpose of AI is not to grant living forever, but to remind us of the preciousness of each moment we're already given.

Chapter 5

Mind-Body Connection and Immortality

What does it truly mean to live forever? For millennia, humanity's pursuit of living forever has centered on preserving the physical body. From the elixirs of ancient alchemy to cutting-edge anti-aging biotechnology, the quest has largely focused on slowing down the aging process, repairing cellular damage, and extending the years of our biological existence. But as modern science advances, a more profound realization is coming to light: living forever may not be achieved by targeting the body alone. The mind—our consciousness, emotions, and thoughts—is a crucial partner in this pursuit.

The mind and body are not separate, isolated entities. Instead, they are interconnected parts of a unified whole, each influencing the other in profound ways. This "mind-body connection" is no longer a mystical or speculative concept. Ground breaking research in fields like neuroscience, psychology, and epigenetics reveals that our mental states—thoughts, emotions, and perceptions—can directly impact our physical health. Chronic stress, for example, accelerates cellular aging by shortening telomeres, the protective caps at the ends of our DNA. On the other hand, practices like mindfulness, meditation, and gratitude have been shown to boost immune function, promote cellular repair, and even influence gene expression. If our goal is not only to live longer but to live better, then mastering this mind-body dynamic is essential.

This chapter delves into how the mind influences the body's ability to heal, regenerate, and endure. We will explore the science of psychoneuroimmunology—the study of how thoughts and emotions impact the immune system—and the potential it holds for human longevity. We'll also examine how emerging technologies, such as brain-computer interfaces (BCIs) and neuroprosthetics, are redefining the boundary between mind and body. These advances hint at a future where our mental processes can directly control our physical state, potentially allowing us to overcome illness, extend life, or even exist beyond the confines of our biological form.

But this interplay is not a one-way street. Just as the mind influences the body, the condition of the body profoundly affects the mind. Cognitive decline caused by neurodegenerative diseases like Alzheimer's and Parkinson's serves as a reminder that a healthy body is essential for maintaining mental clarity and awareness. This relationship has inspired the development of neuroprotective interventions, such as nootropic supplements, brain implants, and AI-powered cognitive training programs. These innovations aim to protect the mind's sharpness and vitality as the body ages, blurring the lines between human potential and technological augmentation.

Interestingly, many of the principles driving the mind-body connection are not new. Ancient systems of knowledge like yoga, meditation, and Ayurveda have long emphasized the unity of mind, body, and spirit. While these traditions were once dismissed as "esoteric" or "non-science-focused," modern research has validated their efficacy. For example, meditation has been shown to reduce stress hormones like cortisol, enhance cognitive performance, and promote emotional well-being. Practices like pranayama (breath control) influence heart rate variability, a key marker of physical resilience. As science catches up with ancient wisdom, we find that the knowledge of the past may hold vital keys to the future of living forever.

So, what does all of this mean for the pursuit of eternal life? Can mastery of the mind-body connection unlock the secret to living forever? The answer lies at the crossroads of science, spirituality, and technology. If the mind can influence the body's capacity to heal and the body can support the mind's longevity, then living forever may not require escaping the human form. Instead, it may demand a deeper understanding of its true potential.

Let us explore several core themes that illuminate the path toward mind-body mastery:

The Science of the Mind-Body Connection:

We'll examine the biological mechanisms that link mental states to physical health. This includes the role of neurotransmitters, hormones, and immune responses in promoting longevity.

Ancient Wisdom Meets Modern Science:

From yogic meditation to breathing exercises, we'll explore the time-tested practices that bridge ancient traditions and modern biomedicine.

The Role of the Immune System:

Known as the body's "internal healer," the immune system plays a pivotal role in longevity. We'll investigate how mental states like stress and calmness impact immune health and how this relationship affects lifespan.

Technological Frontiers of Mind-Body Integration:

We'll look at the revolutionary role of brain-computer interfaces (BCIs), neurofeedback devices, and AI-enhanced cognitive training. Could these tools help us achieve living forever by preserving cognitive function or enabling us to "upload" our minds into digital consciousness?

As we venture into this exploration, prepare to challenge long-held assumptions about human potential. You may discover that living forever does not require transcending the body but rather mastering its connection to the mind. By understanding and harnessing this relationship, we move one step closer to unlocking the ultimate goal: a life without limits, where mind and body work in perfect harmony to defy the constraints of time.

The Science of the Mind-Body Connection

The connection between the mind and the body has long been a topic of fascination and study, bridging ancient wisdom with modern science. This powerful bond reveals that our mental states—thoughts, emotions, and mental well-being—are not isolated from our physical health; rather, they are intricately linked, with profound effects on our longevity and vitality. At the core of this connection lies a intriguing dance of biological mechanisms that allow our thoughts and feelings to influence the very cells of our body.

To begin understanding this connection, it's essential to first explore the role of key players in the mind-body communication: neurotransmitters, hormones, and immune responses. These biochemical messengers serve as the link between the brain and the body, transmitting signals that affect everything from our mood to the health of our organs and tissues.

Neurotransmitters: The Messengers of the Mind:

Neurotransmitters are chemicals in the brain that facilitate communication between neurons, the cells responsible for transmitting information. One of the most well-known neurotransmitters is serotonin, often referred to as the "feel-good" chemical. Serotonin is linked to positive emotions, happiness, and a sense of calm. When serotonin levels are balanced, we feel at peace, our mood stabilizes, and our bodies are better able to recover from stress. In this way, a positive mental state can trigger a cascade of health benefits, including improved immune function and reduced inflammation, both of which are vital for maintaining longevity.

On the other hand, dopamine plays a key role in motivation, pleasure, and reward. Higher dopamine levels are associated with increased energy and a sense of purpose, which can fuel both physical activity and emotional well-being. Maintaining balanced dopamine levels, through activities that promote joy and achievement, can encourage a healthier lifestyle that ultimately supports long-term health.

Hormones: The Body's Internal Regulators:

Hormones, another class of biochemical messengers, are equally powerful in maintaining the mind-body connection. Cortisol, often known as the stress hormone, is one of the most significant players in this interaction. When we are stressed, cortisol levels surge, preparing the body for a fight-or-flight response. While short bursts of cortisol are helpful in moments of danger, chronic stress leads to sustained high cortisol levels, which can wreak havoc on the body. Over time, this can lead to issues such as high blood pressure, weakened immune function, and accelerated cellular aging.

However, just as stress can disrupt our health, oxytocin, the "love hormone," works in the opposite way. Released during moments of bonding, such as hugging or socializing with loved ones, oxytocin has been shown to reduce stress, lower blood pressure, and promote healing. Its role in fostering positive social connections demonstrates how emotional well-being can directly influence our physical health.

The Immune Response: Bridging Mind and Body:

The immune system is one of the most direct ways the mind and body interact. Our mental state can either strengthen or weaken our immune defences. When we experience chronic stress, for example, the body's immune response becomes less effective, leaving us more vulnerable to illness. On the other hand, positive mental health—characterized by optimism, social support, and emotional resilience—can enhance the immune system's ability to fight off infections and promote recovery.

Research shows that mindfulness practices, such as meditation, have a measurable effect on immune function. These practices help reduce the production of pro-inflammatory cytokines, which are linked to various chronic conditions, including cardiovascular disease and arthritis. By calming the mind, we can, in turn, reduce inflammation and improve our body's natural healing processes.

Cellular Aging and the Mind:

Perhaps the most profound connection between the mind and body lies in the process of cellular aging. Each cell in our body contains structures called telomeres, which protect our DNA from damage. As we age, these telomeres shorten, leading to cellular aging and a decline in function. However, research suggests that the state of our mind—particularly our ability to manage stress and cultivate positive emotions—can influence the rate at which our telomeres shorten. Chronic stress accelerates this process, while positive emotions and mindfulness practices seem to slow it down.

In essence, our thoughts, emotions, and mental states are not just abstract experiences; they are deeply embedded in the biological processes that shape our physical health. By nurturing a positive mental environment, managing stress, and cultivating emotional resilience, we are not only improving our quality of life in the present but potentially adding years to our lifespan.

Understanding the science behind the mind-body connection reveals a powerful truth: our mental well-being is directly tied to our physical health. Neurotransmitters like serotonin and dopamine, hormones like cortisol and oxytocin, and the immune system all work together to bridge the mind and body, influencing everything from our mood to our cellular health. By focusing on mental wellness, we can create a profound impact on our longevity, offering the possibility of not just living longer, but living better. The mind and body are not separate entities but are instead two halves of a whole, working in concert to enhance the beauty and vitality of life.

Ancient Wisdom Meets Modern Science

Throughout history, ancient traditions have recognized the profound connection between the mind and body, long before modern science began to understand it. Practices such as yogic meditation and breathing exercises have been used for thousands of years to promote well-being, inner peace, and longevity. Today, as modern biomedicine continues to uncover the biological mechanisms that influence our health, these ancient practices are increasingly validated by science. What was once viewed as mystical or spiritual is now being recognized for its science-focused foundation and its potential to improve our physical and mental health.

In this section, we'll explore how these time-tested techniques, rooted in ancient wisdom, align with modern science-focused findings. By understanding the synergy between the two, we can appreciate how practices like meditation and controlled breathing not only benefit the mind but also enhance physical vitality, support immune function, and may even contribute to longevity.

Yogic Meditation: A Path to Mental and Physical Harmony:

Yoga, particularly meditation, has been a cornerstone of ancient spiritual practices for centuries. But it isn't just about sitting still or chanting mantras. Modern research is now uncovering the science-focused reasons why meditation is so effective at promoting health. One of the most significant findings is the role of meditation in neuroplasticity—the brain's ability to reorganize itself by forming new neural connections. Studies have shown that regular meditation can increase the density of grey matter in areas of the brain involved in memory, learning, and emotional regulation. This leads to improved focus, emotional balance, and resilience to stress.

From a physiological perspective, meditation activates the parasympathetic nervous system, which is responsible for the body's "rest and digest" functions. This reduces the production of stress hormones like cortisol and promotes a state of calm and relaxation. Lower cortisol levels, in turn, help reduce inflammation, lower blood pressure, and improve immune function. The ancient practice of meditation, which was once considered a spiritual discipline, is now understood to be a powerful tool for enhancing overall health.

One of the most popular forms of meditation, mindfulness meditation, has gained widespread recognition in recent years for its mental health benefits. Research has shown that mindfulness can help reduce symptoms of anxiety, depression, and PTSD, while also improving sleep and cognitive function. The deep state of awareness cultivated through mindfulness allows individuals to become more attuned to their thoughts and emotions, leading to better emotional regulation and improved well-being.

Breathing Exercises: Harnessing the Power of the Breath:

Another powerful tool that bridges ancient practices with modern science is pranayama—the practice of controlled breathing in yoga. Ancient yogic texts emphasize the importance of breath control as a means of enhancing life force, or prana. In modern science, we now understand that breathing exercises can influence the autonomic nervous system, which regulates involuntary bodily functions like heart rate, digestion, and respiratory rate. By consciously regulating the breath, we can activate the vagus nerve, which helps shift the body into a state of relaxation and recovery.

One of the most widely practiced pranayama techniques is alternate nostril breathing (Nadi Shodhana), which involves breathing through one nostril at a time while closing the other. This practice is believed to balance the flow of energy within the body and calm the mind. From a science-focused standpoint, this breathing technique has been shown to reduce heart rate, lower blood pressure, and improve brain function. The rhythmic nature of controlled breathing can also help synchronize the body's internal rhythms, promoting a sense of calm and balance.

Deep belly breathing (diaphragmatic breathing) is another powerful pranayama practice that has been studied for its effects on the body's stress response. This type of breathing involves fully expanding the diaphragm as you inhale, allowing the breath to fill the lungs deeply, and exhaling slowly. Research has shown that deep breathing activates the parasympathetic nervous system, which counteracts the effects of stress and promotes relaxation. It also increases oxygen flow to the body, which can improve circulation, support immune function, and enhance overall vitality.

Scientific Validation: The Link between Ancient Practices and Health:

While these practices have been passed down through generations, the modern science-focused community is now beginning to validate their health benefits. A growing body of research supports the idea that ancient techniques like meditation and breathing exercises can enhance both mental and physical health. For example, studies have shown that regular meditation can improve cardiovascular health, reduce inflammation, and enhance the body's ability to manage stress. Similarly, breathing exercises have been found to help regulate blood pressure, improve lung function, and reduce symptoms of anxiety and depression.

One of the most exciting discoveries is the role of these practices in telomere length—the protective caps on the ends of our chromosomes, which shorten as we age. Shortened telomeres are associated with aging and various age-related diseases, but research suggests that mindfulness meditation and breathing exercises may help preserve telomere length, potentially contributing to a longer, healthier life.

A Holistic Approach: Bridging the Mind and Body:

By integrating ancient wisdom with modern science, we gain a more holistic understanding of health. These time-tested practices encourage a deep connection between the mind and body, promoting not only physical well-being but also mental clarity and emotional resilience. Practices like meditation and pranayama help reduce the harmful effects of chronic stress, improve the function of vital systems like the immune and cardiovascular systems, and foster a sense of peace and purpose.

Moreover, the adoption of these practices doesn't require a complete lifestyle overhaul. Even small, consistent efforts—like practicing mindfulness for a few minutes each day or incorporating deep breathing into a daily routine—can lead to significant improvements in both mental and physical health. As modern science continues to uncover the mechanisms behind these ancient practices, we are increasingly able to bridge the gap between mind, body, and spirit.

The intersection of ancient wisdom and modern science offers a powerful approach to well-being. Practices like yogic meditation and breathing exercises are no longer seen as mere spiritual tools but are recognized for their profound effects on our mental and physical health. These techniques, rooted in centuries-old traditions, are now supported by science-focused research, showing that they have the potential to enhance longevity, reduce stress, and improve overall health. By integrating these ancient practices into our modern lives, we can cultivate a deeper sense of balance, vitality, and resilience—helping us lead healthier, longer lives.

The Role of the Immune System

The immune system is often called the body's "internal healer," and for good reason. It works tirelessly to protect us from harmful invaders, such as viruses, bacteria, and other pathogens, all while keeping our body's internal environment in balance. Beyond just defending against disease, the immune system is intimately connected with our overall health and longevity. How well it functions can significantly impact our lifespan, and one of the most fascinating aspects of immune health is how our mental state—whether we are under stress or feeling calm—can directly influence its ability to function.

In this section, we'll explore the powerful connection between the mind and the immune system, showing how mental and emotional states shape our body's ability to heal and thrive. From the damaging effects of chronic stress on immunity to the healing potential of calmness and positive emotions, we'll examine how understanding this relationship can enhance our health and even help us live longer, more vibrant lives.

The Immune System: The Body's First Line of Defence:

The immune system is a intriguing network of cells, tissues, and organs that work together to defend the body against foreign invaders. It is constantly on alert, identifying and neutralizing potential threats, from infections to abnormal cells that could develop into cancer. The system is composed of two main branches: the innate immune system, which provides immediate, nonspecific protection, and the adaptive immune system, which is slower but more targeted, adapting to recognize specific pathogens that the body has encountered before.

In its ideal state, the immune system functions efficiently to protect us from illness while maintaining balance within the body.

However, when the system is weakened or overwhelmed, it becomes less effective at fighting off infections and repairing damage. This is where the mind-body connection comes into play—our mental state can either strengthen or weaken the immune response, making it critical for us to nurture both our physical and emotional health.

Stress and the Immune System: A Dangerous Relationship:

Chronic stress is one of the most damaging factors for immune health. When we experience stress, our body's fight-or-flight response is activated, releasing a flood of hormones like cortisol and adrenaline. While this response is helpful in moments of acute danger, prolonged stress can have a harmful effect on the immune system. Cortisol, the primary stress hormone, suppresses the activity of immune cells, making it more difficult for the body to fight infections or repair cellular damage.

When we are constantly stressed, this immune suppression can lead to a variety of health problems, from frequent colds to more serious conditions like autoimmune diseases and even cancer. Chronic stress also triggers inflammation, a state where the body's immune cells become overactive, attacking healthy cells and tissues. This persistent low-grade inflammation is associated with many age-related diseases, including heart disease, diabetes, and arthritis.

The key problem with chronic stress is that it doesn't just affect the immune system in the short term—it can have lasting impacts. Studies have shown that long-term exposure to stress can shorten telomeres, the protective caps at the ends of our chromosomes, which are crucial for cellular health. As telomeres shorten, cells age more rapidly, and the body becomes more vulnerable to disease. This is one of the ways chronic stress accelerates the aging process and reduces lifespan.

Calmness and Positive Emotions: A Boost for Immunity:

On the other hand, moments of calm and positive emotions can have the opposite effect. Practices like meditation, deep breathing, and mindfulness are known to activate the parasympathetic nervous system, which is responsible for the body's "rest and digest" functions. This state of calm reduces the production of cortisol and allows the immune system to operate at its best.

Research has shown that positive emotions, such as happiness, gratitude, and compassion, can actually boost immune function. For example, studies have found that people who regularly practice gratitude or engage in acts of kindness experience improved immune responses. This is because positive emotions promote the production of endorphins—the body's natural feel-good chemicals—which in turn support immune health by reducing inflammation and improving circulation.

Laughter, too, is a powerful immune booster. It's been shown to increase the production of antibodies and T-cells, which are essential for fighting infections. Laughter reduces stress hormones like cortisol and helps improve overall mood, which in turn strengthens immune function. It's a simple yet effective way to support the body's healing mechanisms and promote a longer, healthier life.

The Power of Mind-Body Practices for Immune Health:

Many ancient practices—such as yoga, tai chi, and breathing exercises—have long been used to foster mental and physical health.

These mind-body practices not only reduce stress but also directly enhance immune function. For example, yogic breathing exercises (pranayama) have been shown to increase lung capacity, reduce stress, and improve blood circulation, all of which support the immune system.

Likewise, tai chi, a practice involving slow, deliberate movements, has been found to reduce inflammation and improve immune responses.

Incorporating these practices into daily life can have a profound impact on immune health. Regular yoga, meditation, or deep-breathing exercises help manage stress, strengthen the body's defence mechanisms, and promote a sense of peace and balance—all of which contribute to longevity. These practices also help regulate the nervous system, preventing it from becoming overstimulated by chronic stress, which in turn keeps the immune system functioning optimally.

The Link between Immune Health and Longevity:

The relationship between the immune system and longevity is clear: a well-functioning immune system is essential for a long and healthy life. When the immune system is strong, it can effectively protect the body from diseases, repair cellular damage, and fight off infections. However, when it is compromised by chronic stress, poor mental health, or a lack of self-care, the body becomes vulnerable to illness, and the aging process accelerates.

Fortunately, we have the power to influence our immune health through our thoughts and emotions. By managing stress, cultivating positive emotions, and engaging in practices that promote mental well-being, we can strengthen our immune system and potentially extend our lifespan. This underscores the importance of adopting a holistic approach to health—one that nourishes both the body and the mind.

The immune system plays a pivotal role in determining how long and how well we live. It is the body's internal healer, constantly at work to protect us from harm. But its ability to function effectively is closely linked to our mental state. Chronic stress can weaken the immune system, leading to a range of health problems and accelerating the aging process. On the other hand, moments of calm, positive emotions, and practices like meditation and yoga can significantly enhance immune health, supporting longevity and vitality.

By understanding the powerful connection between mental well-being and immune function, we can take proactive steps to nurture our health and improve our chances of living a long, healthy life. Cultivating a calm and positive mindset, managing stress, and engaging in immune-boosting activities can not only help us feel better in the present but may also have a lasting impact on our future health. The immune system, after all, is as much a reflection of our internal environment as it is a protector of our external one—and by fostering the right mental state, we can help it fulfil its role as the body's true healer.

Technological Frontiers of Mind-Body Integration:

The mind and body have always been intricately connected, but recent technological advancements are opening new frontiers in how we understand and enhance this connection. Over the past few decades, innovations in fields like brain-computer interfaces (BCIs), neurofeedback devices, and AI-enhanced cognitive training are offering us unprecedented ways to bridge the gap between mind and machine. These technologies hold the potential to not only enhance cognitive function but also offer ground breaking possibilities in extending human life, preserving our mental faculties, and even exploring the controversial concept of "uploading" our consciousness into digital form.

In this section, we will dive into the cutting-edge technologies that are helping us push the boundaries of human potential. Could these advancements lead to living forever, or at least offer a way to preserve our cognitive abilities indefinitely? Let's explore the fascinating ways in which technology is merging with the human mind and body, and how these innovations could redefine what it means to be alive.

Brain-Computer Interfaces: Merging the Mind with Machines:

Brain-computer interfaces (BCIs) are one of the most exciting and transformative technologies of our time. These devices enable direct communication between the brain and external devices, such as computers, prosthetics, or even robotic limbs. By translating neural activity into commands, BCIs bypass the traditional pathways of communication (like muscles or spoken language) and create a direct interface between the brain and technology.

While BCIs have made significant strides in helping people with disabilities regain lost functionality, their potential extends far beyond medical applications. Researchers are exploring how BCIs could be used to enhance cognitive abilities, augment memory, or even allow individuals to control machines or devices with nothing more than their thoughts. Imagine a future where thoughts can directly manipulate technology, or where a person's mental capabilities are boosted with the help of a BCI, increasing cognitive performance and enhancing learning.

One of the more speculative but intriguing possibilities is the use of BCIs to preserve or even extend cognitive function as we age. Could BCIs be used to "upload" memories or mental states into a computer? Or, in the future, could they enable individuals to maintain sharp cognitive abilities long into old age by continuously interfacing with external systems that enhance brain activity? While we are still far from achieving such feats, the groundwork is being laid for what could be a major breakthrough in mind-body integration.

Neurofeedback: Training the Brain for Peak Performance:

Another fascinating technology that is pushing the boundaries of mind-body integration is neurofeedback. Neurofeedback involves using real-time brain activity data to help individuals regulate their brainwave patterns. Through sensors placed on the scalp, a neurofeedback device provides feedback about brain activity, typically displayed through sounds or visuals. This feedback allows users to learn how to modify their brain activity consciously—such as calming an overactive mind or boosting mental focus.

Neurofeedback has already shown promising results in treating conditions like ADHD, anxiety, and PTSD by helping individuals train their brains to function more optimally. But the potential for enhancing cognitive abilities doesn't stop there. Research suggests that neurofeedback could be used to improve memory, concentration, and emotional regulation. Over time, consistent training may lead to long-term changes in the brain's structure and function, enhancing mental well-being and performance.

As our understanding of neurofeedback deepens, it's possible that this technology could also play a role in preserving cognitive function in older adults. By continuously training the brain, we might be able to stave off cognitive decline, reduce the risk of diseases like

Alzheimer's, and even slow the process of brain aging. The prospect of using neurofeedback to optimize brain function for longevity—ensuring a sharper, more agile mind well into the later years of life—could be a revolutionary step toward enhancing human lifespan.

AI-Enhanced Cognitive Training: A New Era of Brain Optimization:

Artificial intelligence (AI) is another rapidly advancing field that holds incredible potential for mind-body integration. AI-driven cognitive training programs are already being used to enhance various aspects of mental performance, from memory and attention to problem-solving and creativity. These AI programs are designed to adapt to the individual user's needs, offering personalized exercises and challenges based on real-time feedback.

What makes AI so powerful in this context is its ability to analyse vast amounts of data and customize training programs to an individual's cognitive strengths and weaknesses. As these systems become more sophisticated, AI could offer increasingly effective ways to optimize brain function. For example, AI could be used to identify patterns in cognitive decline and offer early interventions, potentially preventing or slowing conditions like dementia. Additionally, AI-powered cognitive training might allow individuals to enhance their mental agility, creativity, and learning ability, leading to a more fulfilling and intellectually vibrant life.

In terms of longevity, AI's potential to preserve cognitive function is particularly exciting. By continuously enhancing and optimizing brain performance, AI could help maintain sharpness and clarity well into advanced age. Cognitive training powered by AI might one day allow individuals to maintain a mental "edge" throughout their lives, helping to ensure that our minds remain just as youthful as our bodies.

Uploading Consciousness: The Digital Dream (or Nightmare?):

One of the most ambitious and futuristic ideas that has captured the imagination of researchers and futurists alike is the concept of uploading consciousness—the idea that our minds could be transferred or "uploaded" into a digital form, allowing us to live indefinitely in a virtual or artificial environment. This concept, often referred to as mind uploading or whole brain emulation, suggests that if we could map the human brain in its entirety and recreate its functions in a digital environment, it might be possible to preserve our consciousness beyond the physical limitations of the body.

While this idea may sound like science fiction, advancements in neuroimaging, artificial intelligence, and BCIs are gradually making it more plausible. The fundamental challenge lies in fully understanding how the brain encodes thoughts, memories, and consciousness itself. If we can map and replicate the brain's neural structure and activity on a computer, we could, in theory, upload our minds to a machine that could exist independently of the biological body.

However, there are many technical, ethical, and thought-provoking challenges to this idea. For one, it's still unclear whether a digital version of a person would truly be "you," or simply a replica of your consciousness. Furthermore, there are profound ethical concerns regarding the implications of living forever through digital consciousness—what does it mean to be human, and how would society navigate issues of identity, rights, and continuity of life in a virtual world?

The Future of Mind-Body Integration:

As technology continues to advance, the line between mind and body is becoming increasingly blurred. Brain-computer interfaces, neurofeedback devices, and AI-enhanced cognitive training represent just the beginning of a new era of mind-body integration. These technologies hold the potential to revolutionize how we understand and preserve cognitive function, and could even offer a pathway to extending human life by enhancing our mental abilities and preserving our consciousness.

While we are still a long way from achieving living forever or fully uploading our minds into digital form, the progress being made in these fields is undeniably exciting. As we move forward, it will be crucial to explore the ethical, thought-provoking, and societal implications of these technologies, ensuring that we use them in ways that enhance human well-being and dignity. But one thing is clear: the future of mind-body integration promises a radical reimagining of human potential, offering new possibilities for longevity, cognitive enhancement, and perhaps even the very nature of life itself

Yoga and Meditation: A Path to Spiritual Longevity

For millennia, humanity has pursued health, wisdom, and a deeper understanding of existence. Among the most profound and enduring methods for achieving these goals are the ancient practices of yoga and meditation. Rooted in India's rich spiritual heritage, these disciplines offer far more than physical well-being. They serve as pathways to mental clarity, emotional balance, and spiritual liberation. But could they also hold the key to longevity—not just in terms of years lived but in the depth, quality, and spiritual fulfilment of those years?

Yoga and meditation are not merely exercises or stress-relief techniques. They are transformative practices that bridge the mind and body, fostering a profound state of harmony. Modern science is now catching up with what ancient sages understood intuitively: the mind's state shapes the body's health and longevity. Emerging research in neuroscience, psychology, and epigenetics reveals that yoga and meditation can influence cellular health, immune function, and even genetic expression—all factors linked to aging and lifespan.

In this section, we explore the philosophy, science, and transformative potential of yoga and meditation. We'll examine how these practices nurture longevity, deepen spiritual awareness, and challenge conventional views of mortality. By integrating ancient wisdom with modern science, we'll uncover how yoga and meditation might not only extend our years but also imbue them with purpose, vitality, and inner peace.

The Philosophy of Yoga and Meditation

At their heart, yoga and meditation seek to dissolve the perceived boundaries between mind and body, revealing the interconnected nature of all existence. The term "yoga" means "union" in Sanskrit—the unification of the self with the greater whole. This holistic state of balance is seen as essential for physical health, mental clarity, and spiritual growth. The ultimate goal of this practice is "moksha," or liberation from the cycle of birth, death, and rebirth.

Key Concepts of Yoga:

Asana:

(Physical Postures): Asanas are more than physical exercises; they prepare the body to sit comfortably in meditation for extended periods. Poses like "Trikonasana" (triangle pose) promote strength, flexibility, and balance—qualities essential for long-term health.

Pranayama:

(Breath Control): The breath is the bridge between the mind and body. Pranayama practices like Nadi Shodhana (alternate nostril breathing) balance the nervous system, reduce stress, and increase mental clarity, which supports longevity.

Dhyana (Meditation):

Dhyana is the state of deep, unbroken concentration that transcends ordinary thought. It's the bridge to "Samadhi" (absorption), where the sense of individual self dissolves into a state of oneness.

Samadhi (Blissful Absorption):

The ultimate goal of yoga, Samadhi is the experience of unity with the infinite. It's in this state that practitioners are said to glimpse the timeless and eternal nature of existence.

Key Concepts of Meditation:

Mindfulness Meditation:

Focuses on being present, observing thoughts and sensations without judgment. This practice promotes emotional resilience and reduces stress, both critical factors for longevity.

Loving-Kindness Meditation (Metta):

This practice cultivates compassion and love for oneself and others, which supports emotional well-being and strengthens social bonds, both of which have been linked to increased lifespan.

Transcendental Meditation:

By repeating a mantra, the mind enters a deep state of restful awareness, which reduces stress, enhances cognitive function, and promotes mental clarity.

These practices, rooted in ancient philosophy, aim to cultivate an enduring sense of peace and self-realization. The timeless wisdom they offer extends far beyond mere physical survival—it opens the path to spiritual living forever.

Scientific Foundations of Yoga and Meditation

In recent years, modern science has validated the profound effects of yoga and meditation on the mind and body. No longer seen as "alternative" wellness practices, they are now backed by research in neuroscience, psychology, and molecular biology. Their impact goes beyond relaxation—they induce measurable changes in brain structure, gene expression, and cellular health.

Neuroplasticity and Brain Health:

Neurogenesis:

Studies show that meditation increases grey matter density in areas of the brain responsible for memory, learning, and emotional regulation. This supports cognitive longevity and reduces the risk of neurodegenerative diseases like Alzheimer's and Parkinson's.

Mind-Body Synchronization:

Practices like pranayama stimulate the vagus nerve, which activates the parasympathetic nervous system, promoting relaxation and stress reduction. Chronic stress, as we know, accelerates cellular aging.

Hormonal Balance and Stress Reduction:

Reduction of Cortisol ("Stress Hormone"):

Prolonged stress shortens telomeres—the protective caps on DNA—accelerating aging. Meditation reduces cortisol levels, thereby slowing telomere shortening and promoting longevity.

Increase in Serotonin and Dopamine:

These neurotransmitters are linked to happiness, motivation, and emotional stability. Their increase through meditation promotes mental well-being and a positive outlook on life, which supports long-term health.

Epigenetic Effects on Longevity:

Gene Expression:

Research suggests that yoga and meditation can influence the expression of genes linked to inflammation, immune function, and stress response. This process, known as epigenetics, reveals how lifestyle changes can "turn on" genes that support health and "turn off" those linked to disease.

Telomere Preservation:

Regular meditation has been shown to maintain telomere length, effectively "adding years" to a person's biological age.

3. Practical Techniques for Longevity

The power of yoga and meditation lies not in theory but in practice. Consistency and intention are key to unlocking their full potential. Here are practical techniques to incorporate into daily life for health and longevity.

Yoga Techniques for Longevity:

Savasana (Corpse Pose):

Often practiced at the end of a yoga session, this pose promotes deep relaxation, helping the body enter a restorative state essential for longevity.

Adho Mukha Svanasana (Downward Dog):

This pose improves circulation and lymphatic drainage, essential for cellular health.

Pranayama Techniques:

Alternate nostril breathing (Nadi Shodhana) calms the mind, while Kapalabhati (skull-shining breath) detoxifies the body and increases vitality.

Meditation Techniques for Longevity:

Mindfulness Practice:

10-20 minutes of daily mindfulness meditation can reduce stress, boost immune function, and enhance emotional stability.

Metta (Loving-Kindness) Meditation:

This practice cultivates compassion and fosters social connection—a key factor linked to increased lifespan.

4. Spiritual Implications of Longevity

While physical health is important, yoga and meditation also point toward a deeper form of living forever—spiritual living forever. This concept challenges our understanding of time, death, and the self.

The Role of Self-Realization:

Atman and Immortality:

In yogic philosophy, "Atman" refers to the eternal self or soul, which is distinct from the body. Recognizing this eternal self leads to spiritual liberation (moksha), which some interpret as the ultimate form of living forever.

Transcending Time and Space:

In deep meditative states, practitioners report experiencing "timeless awareness" that hints at the infinite nature of existence.

Reincarnation and the Karmic Cycle:

Breaking the Cycle of Rebirth:

Spiritual wisdom, achieved through yoga and meditation, is believed to free the soul from the cycle of birth and rebirth (samsara), offering liberation (moksha).

Yoga and meditation offer more than physical health—they provide a path to holistic longevity. From stress reduction and neurogenesis to the preservation of telomeres, these practices influence the very building blocks of life. Yet, they also challenge us to see longevity as more than survival. They point toward liberation, transcendence, and self-realization. Perhaps, true living forever lies not in defying death but in mastering life, moment by moment, breath by breath.

The Power of the Mind: Can Thoughts Influence Lifespan?

What if the secret to a longer life resided not in pills, diets, or technological innovations, but in the very thoughts that occupy our minds? While this notion may seem like a concept rooted in spiritual philosophy, modern science is beginning to catch up. Our thoughts—both conscious and subconscious—hold profound power over our physical health, affecting everything from the immune system to cellular aging. This section explores the emerging science behind how thoughts, beliefs, and mental states may influence lifespan, offering a fascinating perspective on the mind-body connection.

From the placebo effect to the biology of belief, research suggests that the mind's influence on the body is more profound than previously imagined. Positive thoughts can stimulate the production of "feel-good" neurotransmitters and hormones that promote well-being, while chronic negative thinking is linked to stress, inflammation, and disease. Could mastering our thoughts be a key to unlocking longevity? We'll explore this possibility, weaving together insights from psychology, neuroscience, and ancient wisdom.

The Biology of Belief

One of the most compelling arguments for the power of thought on physical health comes from the "biology of belief," a concept popularized by cell biologist Dr. Bruce Lipton. According to Lipton's work, beliefs and perceptions are not passive mental states—they actively shape the body's biochemistry.

The Role of Perception in Cellular Function:

Cellular Receptors and Environmental Signals: Our cells have receptors that respond to chemical signals from the brain. When we experience stress or fear, the brain releases cortisol and adrenaline, which prepare the body for a fight-or-flight response. While useful in short bursts, chronic stress floods the body with these hormones, causing wear and tear at the cellular level.

Epigenetic Changes:

Beliefs and mental states can influence gene expression. Stress-related thoughts, for instance, can activate genes that promote inflammation, while positive mental states may activate genes linked to longevity and resilience.

The Placebo Effect: Belief as Medicine:

The placebo effect demonstrates that belief alone can trigger real physiological changes. When patients believe they're receiving effective treatment—even if it's a sugar pill—their symptoms often improve. This "mind over matter" phenomenon highlights the body's innate capacity to heal itself under the influence of thought.

How Positive Thinking Affects Longevity

Research indicates that optimism and positive thinking are not just feel-good platitudes—they're predictors of longer, healthier lives.

Key Scientific Findings:

- The "Nun Study": A famous longitudinal study of Catholic nuns found that those who expressed positive emotions and optimism in their early autobiographical writings lived, on average, seven to ten years longer than their less positive peers.
- Longevity Studies on Optimism: A 2019 study published in PNAS (Proceedings of the National Academy of Sciences) concluded that people with higher levels of optimism had an 11-15% longer lifespan, with an increased likelihood of living past 85.

Mechanisms of Positive Thinking:

Reduced Cortisol Levels:

Positive thoughts counteract stress responses, reducing cortisol production. Chronic stress accelerates cellular aging by shortening telomeres—the protective caps on the ends of chromosomes. Positive thinking may slow telomere shortening, thereby slowing the aging process.

Increased Oxytocin and Endorphins:

Positive mental states boost the release of oxytocin and endorphins, hormones associated with love, bonding, and happiness. These chemicals reduce inflammation and promote healing at the cellular level.

Resilience to Adversity:

Optimistic people tend to cope better with adversity, which protects them from chronic stress and its negative health effects.

The Dark Side: How Negative Thoughts Shorten Lifespan

Just as positive thoughts can extend life, negative thoughts can have the opposite effect. Chronic negative mental states—like anxiety, pessimism, and unresolved trauma—create conditions that accelerate aging.

The Impact of Chronic Stress on Aging:

Cortisol and Telomere Shortening:

Chronic stress floods the body with cortisol, which, over time, leads to oxidative stress and inflammation. This process accelerates telomere shortening, effectively "aging" our cells.

Inflammation and Disease:

Negative thoughts increase pro-inflammatory cytokines, chemicals that drive chronic inflammation. Over time, this inflammation contributes to conditions like cardiovascular disease, diabetes, and neurodegeneration.

Negative Thought Loops:

The Role of Rumination:

People who "ruminate" or replay negative thoughts repeatedly are at higher risk of developing anxiety, depression, and stress-related illnesses. Rumination keeps the body's stress response system in a constant state of activation, impairing the immune system and cognitive function.

Can We Train Our Thoughts to Live Longer?

If thoughts can influence lifespan, it raises an exciting question: Can we train our minds to think in ways that promote longevity? Techniques like mindfulness meditation, cognitive behavioural therapy (CBT), and mental conditioning exercises provide powerful tools to reframe negative thought patterns and cultivate positive mental states.

Mindfulness Meditation:

Present-Moment Awareness:

Mindfulness meditation trains the mind to focus on the present moment, reducing rumination and worry. Studies have shown that long-term meditation practice increases grey matter density in the brain and reduces the activity of the amygdala—the "fear centre" of the brain.

Emotional Regulation:

Mindfulness promotes emotional regulation, reducing the impact of negative emotions on health and aging.

Cognitive Behavioural Therapy (CBT):

Reprogramming Negative Thought Patterns:

CBT is a structured approach to identifying and challenging negative thought patterns. It's used to treat anxiety, depression, and PTSD—all of which have been linked to poorer health outcomes.

Empowering Positivity:

By reprogramming the mind's "default" thought patterns, CBT empowers people to think more optimistically and adopt healthier mental habits.

Neuroplasticity and Mental Conditioning:

Brain's Ability to Rewire Itself:

The brain's neuroplasticity—its ability to rewire itself—means that our thoughts can change over time. By repeatedly engaging in positive thinking exercises, gratitude journaling, and mental affirmations, individuals can "train" their minds to focus on positivity, much like training a muscle.

The Role of Spirituality and Belief Systems

For centuries, spiritual traditions have emphasized the power of thought to shape reality. From the yogic concept of "sankalpa" (intentional resolve) to Christian teachings on faith and belief, many wisdom traditions suggest that our inner world determines our outer experience.

Spiritual Longevity Practices:

Visualization and Intention Setting:

Spiritual practices often emphasize visualizing positive outcomes and setting intentions. These mental "seeds" are believed to manifest into physical reality over time.

Belief in a Higher Power:

Studies have shown that people with strong spiritual beliefs have longer lifespans, possibly due to reduced anxiety about death, greater social support, and increased mental resilience.

The power of thought extends far beyond the mind—it reaches into the body, influencing health, aging, and even longevity. Positive mental states can protect against disease, enhance cellular health, and even extend lifespan, while negative thoughts have the opposite effect.

By mastering our thoughts through practices like mindfulness, meditation, and cognitive reprogramming, we can take an active role in our health and longevity. The age-old adage "You become what you think" may be more than thought-provoking wisdom—it may be a science-focused truth. Every great transformation begins with a single thought, and in the pursuit of living forever, our minds may hold the key.

Physical Health and Mental Well-being: A Holistic Approach to Life Extension

What if the key to life extension wasn't hidden in futuristic technologies, anti-aging drugs, or genetic modifications? What if it lay in the choices we make every single day—the food we eat, the way we move, and even the thoughts we think? As it turns out, science is revealing that physical health and mental well-being are deeply intertwined, forming a powerful foundation for both healthspan (the years of life spent in good health) and lifespan (the total years lived).

A truly holistic approach to longevity looks beyond isolated hacks or miracle treatments. It emphasizes the profound connections between the body, mind, and spirit. From mindful living and balanced nutrition to movement and emotional well-being, this chapter explores how a unified approach can help us live longer and live better. By integrating ancient wisdom with modern science, we'll see that the path to longevity is not just about adding years to life—it's about adding life to those years.

The Interdependence of Physical and Mental Health

The ancient adage "A healthy mind in a healthy body" reflects a truth that modern research is increasingly confirming. Our physical health and mental well-being are not separate entities—they are deeply interconnected. A calm, focused mind strengthens the immune system, while a strong, active body supports mental clarity and emotional balance. But how do these systems work together?

How the Mind Affects the Body:

Stress and Inflammation:

Chronic stress releases cortisol, a hormone that prepares the body for "fight or flight." While helpful in short bursts, prolonged exposure to cortisol increases inflammation, which accelerates aging and raises the risk of heart disease, diabetes, and cognitive decline.

The Placebo Effect:

Belief alone can produce physiological changes. Studies show that patients who believe they're receiving effective treatment often experience real improvements in symptoms. This "mind-over-matter" effect demonstrates how mental states directly influence physical health.

Mental Health's Role in Immunity:

Optimism, emotional well-being, and resilience are linked to a stronger immune system. On the other hand, anxiety and depression suppress immune responses, making the body more susceptible to disease.

How the Body Affects the Mind:

Exercise and Neurogenesis:

Regular physical activity boosts the production of brain-derived neurotrophic factor (BDNF), a protein that promotes the growth of new neurons. This supports learning, memory, and cognitive health as we age.

Nutrition's Impact on Mood:

Diets rich in omega-3 fatty acids, whole grains, fruits, and vegetables enhance mental clarity and emotional well-being. Diets high in sugar and processed foods, by contrast, have been linked to anxiety, depression, and cognitive decline.

The Gut-Brain Axis:

The gut and brain communicate via the vagus nerve. A healthy gut microbiome, shaped by a fibre-rich diet, has been linked to better emotional regulation and cognitive performance.

Physical Health Strategies for Life Extension

Many life extension strategies focus on physical health—and for good reason. Our lifestyle choices directly affect how well our cells age and how resistant we are to disease. Here's how we can optimize our physical health for longevity.

Exercise and Movement:

Aerobic Exercise:

Activities like walking, running, and swimming enhance heart health, improve mitochondrial function, and increase brain-derived neurotrophic factor (BDNF), which supports brain health.

Resistance Training:

Strength training builds muscle mass and bone density, reducing the risk of frailty as we age. It's crucial for preventing the falls and injuries that often shorten lifespan in older adults.

Flexibility and Balance:

Practices like yoga and tai chi improve balance, coordination, and flexibility. These activities reduce injury risk and enhance the mind-body connection.

Nutrition and Diet:

Caloric Restriction (CR):

Consuming fewer calories while maintaining nutrient intake has been shown to slow aging in animal models. Human studies suggest similar benefits, such as reduced inflammation and improved metabolic health.

Intermittent Fasting:

This practice activates autophagy—a "cellular cleanup" process that removes damaged cellular components. Autophagy plays a critical role in anti-aging and disease prevention.

Nutrient-Dense Diets:

Diets like the Mediterranean diet emphasize whole foods, healthy fats, and plant-based nutrition. These diets have been linked to reduced inflammation, cardiovascular health, and cognitive longevity.

Sleep Hygiene:

Quality over Quantity:

While 7-9 hours of sleep is ideal, the quality of sleep matters most. Deep sleep stages help repair tissues, consolidate memories, and flush out toxins from the brain.

Circadian Rhythm Synchronization:

Exposure to natural light during the day and limiting blue light at night optimizes sleep-wake cycles, supporting overall metabolic health and mental clarity.

Mental Well-Being Strategies for Life Extension

Physical health alone isn't enough for longevity. Mental health is equally crucial, affecting everything from immune function to cognitive aging. Here's how to strengthen mental well-being for life extension.

Stress Management:

Mindfulness and Meditation:

Meditation reduces amygdala activity (the brain's fear centre) and increases grey matter density. Long-term practice enhances emotional regulation and reduces anxiety.

Breathwork:

Techniques like pranayama activate the parasympathetic nervous system, promoting relaxation and reducing heart rate. This practice calms the mind and supports heart health.

Social Connection and Emotional Health:

The Power of Relationships:

People with strong social ties have a lower risk of mortality. Emotional support reduces stress, and positive social interactions increase oxytocin, the "bonding hormone," which promotes longevity.

Gratitude and Positivity:

Journaling about gratitude promotes optimism, which has been linked to reduced disease risk. Positive emotions stimulate the release of feel-good hormones like dopamine and serotonin.

Cognitive Training:

Brain Plasticity:

The brain's ability to change over time (neuroplasticity) allows for lifelong learning. Engaging in challenging cognitive activities like puzzles, language learning, and musical training supports cognitive health.

Memory and Focus Training:

Memory-enhancing techniques like mnemonics and "deep work" sessions strengthen attention and mental clarity, especially as we age.

Holistic Life Extension Practices

A holistic approach to life extension integrates physical and mental health. It's not enough to eat well or meditate in isolation. Synergy between body and mind is essential for sustainable longevity.

Daily Rituals for Longevity:

Morning Rituals:

Start the day with meditation, breathwork, and movement (like yoga or walking) to reduce stress and cultivate mental clarity.

Evening Rituals:

Reduce blue light exposure, engage in gratitude journaling, and use relaxation techniques to promote restorative sleep.

Spirituality's Role in Longevity:

Purpose and Meaning: Research shows that a strong sense of purpose reduces mortality risk. People who find "ikigai" (a Japanese concept for life's purpose) live longer, healthier lives.

Transcendence and Mindfulness:

Spiritual practices like prayer, service, and reflection offer a sense of peace and fulfilment, which buffers against the negative effects of stress.

The pursuit of longevity is not just about science—it's about lifestyle, purpose, and balance. Physical health and mental well-being are not separate; they are two sides of the same coin. By integrating exercise, nutrition, mindfulness, emotional connection, and cognitive resilience, we create a holistic strategy for life extension.

The dream of living forever may be beyond our reach, but a longer, healthier, and more meaningful life is well within it. By taking a holistic approach, we don't just add years to our lives—we add life to our years. As science evolves, one truth remains clear: true longevity is not a technological race, but a human endeavour rooted in timeless principles of wellness, purpose, and love.

Neuroplasticity: Rewiring the Brain for a Longer, Healthier Life

For centuries, the human brain was thought to be a fixed, unchanging organ—its growth and development limited to childhood. But modern neuroscience has upended this belief. The brain, as it turns out, is incredibly adaptable throughout life. This capacity for change is known as neuroplasticity—our brain's remarkable ability to reorganize itself by forming new neural connections in response to experiences, learning, and even injury.

Beyond learning new skills or recovering from trauma, neuroplasticity has profound implications for longevity. By enhancing cognitive flexibility, emotional resilience, and mental sharpness, neuroplasticity contributes to both healthspan (the period of life spent in good health) and lifespan (total years lived). This section delves into the science behind neuroplasticity, its role in life extension, and practical ways to activate it for a longer, healthier life.

What is Neuroplasticity?

Neuroplasticity is the brain's ability to change its structure, functions, and neural pathways in response to learning, experience, or injury. It's a dynamic process that involves both the creation of new synapses (synaptogenesis) and the elimination of old, unused connections (synaptic pruning). While neuroplasticity is most active during childhood, it's now well established that adults, too, can "rewire" their brains at any age.

Types of Neuroplasticity:

Structural Plasticity:

Changes in the brain's physical structure, such as the growth of new synapses or the formation of new neural pathways.

Functional Plasticity:

The brain's ability to shift functions from one area to another, often observed after brain injuries like strokes.

How Neuroplasticity Works:

Imagine your brain's neural pathways as hiking trails through a forest. The more frequently a trail is used, the more well-defined it becomes. Conversely, trails that aren't used often get overgrown. This is how neural pathways work—repeated thoughts, actions, or habits strengthen neural connections, while unused ones are pruned away. This process governs learning, memory, and emotional regulation, all of which play a role in overall longevity.

The Role of Neuroplasticity in Longevity

Neuroplasticity's impact on longevity extends far beyond cognitive skills. It also influences emotional well-being, stress resilience, and physical health. Together, these factors contribute to a longer, healthier life.

Cognitive Longevity:

Memory Retention:

Engaging in activities that boost neuroplasticity, like learning new languages or playing musical instruments, helps maintain memory. Neuroplasticity supports the formation and retrieval of memories, potentially delaying cognitive decline, Alzheimer's, and dementia.

Problem-Solving and Adaptability:

With age, problem-solving can become more challenging. However, neuroplasticity allows for cognitive adaptability, enabling older adults to approach challenges with fresh perspectives and creative solutions.

Emotional and Mental Health:

Stress Management:

Chronic stress increases the activity of the amygdala (the brain's "fear centre") while shrinking the hippocampus (the memory centre). Neuroplasticity-driven interventions, such as mindfulness meditation, can reverse these effects, promoting emotional balance.

Emotional Resilience:

Emotional trauma and chronic stress can reinforce negative emotional loops. By using techniques like cognitive behavioural therapy (CBT), individuals can "rewire" their emotional responses, fostering healthier thought patterns.

Physical Health and Longevity:

Motor Skills and Mobility:

Declines in motor skills with age can be mitigated by neuroplasticity. Practices like tai chi, dance, and balance training improve motor control, reducing the risk of falls and injuries—a critical factor in healthy aging.

Brain-Body Connection:

The brain's plasticity influences bodily systems like the immune system and gut-brain axis. A healthier, more "plastic" brain promotes better immune responses and overall physical health.

Neuroplasticity and Aging: Myths and Realities

Myth 1: The Brain Stops Changing After Childhood:

Reality: Neuroplasticity continues throughout life. New neurons (a process called neurogenesis) form in the hippocampus, and adults can create new neural connections in response to learning, experiences, and challenges.

Myth 2: Cognitive Decline is Inevitable with Age:

Reality: While aging does bring changes in cognitive function, cognitive decline is not inevitable. Neuroplasticity can slow, halt, or even reverse age-related cognitive decline through mental stimulation, physical exercise, and social engagement.

Myth 3: "Use it or lose it" is an Oversimplification:

Reality: While disused neural pathways are "pruned," it's possible to revive dormant areas of the brain. New skills, challenging tasks, and social interaction can reactivate and strengthen these pathways.

Practical Ways to Harness Neuroplasticity for Longevity

Mental Stimulation:

Learn New Skills:

Take up a new language, instrument, or creative hobby like painting or coding. New learning experiences create fresh neural connections.

Puzzles and Games:

Activities like Sudoku, chess, and crosswords engage problem-solving and logic, promoting neurogenesis and cognitive resilience.

Mindfulness and Meditation:

Mindfulness Meditation:

Increases grey matter density in areas linked to emotional regulation and learning.

Breathwork and Pranayama:

Breathing techniques activate the vagus nerve, promoting relaxation and emotional stability.

Physical Exercise:

Aerobic Exercise:

Running, swimming, and other aerobic activities increase brain-derived neurotrophic factor (BDNF), a key protein for neuroplasticity.

Coordination Activities:

Tai chi and balance training improve motor control, reduce injury risk, and maintain physical health.

Nutrition and Brain Health:

Omega-3 Fatty Acids:

Found in fish, walnuts, and flaxseeds, omega-3s support brain health by aiding in the formation of cell membranes.

Antioxidants and Polyphenols:

Foods like berries, green tea, and dark chocolate protect brain cells from oxidative stress, a major driver of aging.

Social Engagement:

Deep Conversations:

Engaging in thoughtful discussions challenges cognitive and emotional flexibility.

Community Involvement:

Volunteering and social engagement stimulate mental activity and emotional well-being.

Neuroplasticity's Role in the Quest for Immortality

As humanity strives to extend life through technology and biology, neuroplasticity offers a "low-tech" but profoundly effective approach. Unlike gene editing or experimental drugs, neuroplasticity is accessible to everyone. By actively rewiring our brains, we can slow cognitive decline, boost emotional resilience, and improve physical health—all of which contribute to a longer, more fulfilling life.

Neuroplasticity also plays a pivotal role in the concept of "digital living forever," where a person's thoughts, habits, and personality are preserved through AI models. By understanding how human thought patterns are formed and changed, researchers can more accurately simulate the minds of real people in digital form, pushing the boundaries of what it means to live on after death.

Neuroplasticity is a profound reminder that we are not prisoners of our biology. Our brains can grow, change, and evolve throughout life. By engaging in activities that challenge the mind, support emotional health, and promote physical wellness, we can harness neuroplasticity to extend both health span and lifespan. The future of life extension isn't only in laboratories or silicon chips—it's in our ability to rewire our brains, one new connection at a time.

Chapter 6

The Psychology of Death and Immortality

Death is life's most profound certainty and, paradoxically, its greatest mystery. For centuries, philosophers, spiritual leaders, and scientists have grappled with questions surrounding mortality: What does it mean to die? How should we live in the face of inevitable death? And perhaps the most audacious question of all—can we overcome it?

This chapter delves into the psychology of death and living forever, exploring how the human mind perceives, fears, and rationalizes its own end. Death is more than a biological event; it is a psychological experience that shapes human identity, drives culture, and influences our deepest decisions. Our relationship with mortality impacts everything—from the pursuit of legacy and meaning to the rise of living forever-focused technologies.

But as we edge closer to the possibility of life extension or even "digital living forever," our psychological framework for understanding death faces an unprecedented shift. If death is no longer an absolute endpoint, how do our beliefs, fears, and motivations evolve? Do we become liberated or imprisoned by the promise of unending existence?

Here we will explore these existential questions, beginning with the psychological foundations of death awareness and how it has shaped human evolution, culture, and behaviour. We will then examine humanity's changing attitudes toward living forever—

tracing the arc from ancient religious beliefs to modern technological ambitions. Finally, we will reflect on the psychological implications of a world where death is no longer certain, where living forever—or something like it—is within reach.

Death Anxiety and the Human Condition

The fear of death, also known as "thanatophobia," is one of the most universal human experiences. Unlike other species, humans possess the unique ability to imagine their own future demise, a consequence of our advanced prefrontal cortex and capacity for abstract thought. This awareness of death—known as "mortality salience"—has a profound impact on our mental health, daily choices, and worldview.

Terror Management Theory (TMT) suggests that our awareness of mortality motivates us to seek meaning, significance, and symbolic living forever. By embedding ourselves in enduring cultural institutions—such as religion, art, and legacy-building—we shield ourselves from the existential terror of nonexistence. This theory explains why people pursue wealth, fame, family legacies, and creative works that "outlive" their physical bodies.

But what happens if death is no longer a certainty? If the concept of death shifts from "inevitable" to "optional," will we lose the motivational force that drives human ambition and creativity? This question lies at the heart of the modern living forever debate.

Cultural Perspectives on Death and Immortality

Throughout history, different cultures have conceptualized death and living forever in diverse ways. From the ancient Egyptians' obsession with mummification to the Hindu belief in reincarnation, human beings have always sought to transcend death in some form.

Ancient Beliefs and Rituals:

Early civilizations viewed death as a transitional phase, a journey to another world. The concept of an "afterlife" provided psychological comfort, easing the fear of oblivion. Egyptian tombs, Norse Valhalla, and Christian heaven are all examples of symbolic living forever—where one's soul or consciousness continues beyond the physical body.

Eastern vs. Western Views:

Eastern philosophies such as Hinduism and Buddhism emphasize the cyclical nature of life and death. Reincarnation, or "samsara," frames death as a necessary stage in a larger spiritual journey. In contrast, many Western ideologies—shaped by Christianity and materialism—view death as a final end, with the promise of an eternal afterlife or "salvation" for the righteous.

Modern Perspectives:

Today's perspectives on death are evolving as science and technology challenge long-standing beliefs. Cryonics, AI-based "mind uploading," and anti-aging biotechnology introduce a secular alternative to religious afterlife beliefs. These new paradigms are not just technological; they are profoundly psychological, reconfiguring our relationship with mortality.

As living forever becomes a possibility, modern humans must confront a new question: If we can extend life indefinitely, will the desire for symbolic living forever—like legacy-building—fade, or will it evolve into new forms?

Immortality's Psychological Allure

Why do we chase living forever? Is it purely a survival instinct, or is it fuelled by something deeper—perhaps the desire for meaning, control, or mastery over nature?

Psychologists have identified several motivations for pursuing living forever:

Control over the Unknown:

Mortality represents the ultimate "unknown," and control is a core psychological need. If technology offers mastery over death, it satisfies our desire to conquer uncertainty.

Fear of Nonexistence:

For many, the idea of "ceasing to exist" is the most terrifying part of death. Technologies like cryonics and mind-uploading address this fear directly, promising continuity of consciousness.

Desire for Mastery:

Humans have always sought to "conquer nature" through exploration, invention, and technology. Immortality—as the ultimate conquest—is a natural extension of this drive.

Desire for Legacy:

People yearn to be remembered. If physical living forever becomes possible, the need for symbolic living forever (like writing books or creating art) may evolve into something else: the pursuit of personal, ongoing influence over future generations.

Psychological Challenges of Immortality

If humans achieve physical living forever or mind-uploading, we may face psychological challenges that current generations cannot fully imagine. The concept of "eternal life" may seem appealing in theory, but it presents unique mental, emotional, and existential dilemmas:

Existential Boredom:

If life stretches on endlessly, how do we maintain purpose, curiosity, and excitement? Some philosophers warn that an infinite life could lead to "eternal boredom," as every possible experience is eventually exhausted.

Loss of Urgency and Motivation:

Much of our motivation to achieve, create, and take risks is rooted in the knowledge that "life is short." Without death as a deadline, will human ambition diminish, or will it evolve into something new?

Identity Crisis:

If we constantly "upgrade" our consciousness through mind-uploading or body replacement, how do we maintain a coherent sense of self? Who are we, if our physical body—the core of human identity—is constantly changing?

These psychological hurdles present profound challenges. They suggest that while living forever may solve one set of fears (fear of death), it introduces new ones (fear of stagnation, loss of meaning, and loss of identity).

The Paradox of Mortality and Meaning

Is it possible that death—despite being our greatest fear—is also essential for meaning? The knowledge that life is finite compels us to live fully, prioritize relationships, and pursue dreams. Without mortality, the human condition may transform in ways we have yet to comprehend.

Some argue that the awareness of death—not its avoidance—is the true key to a meaningful life. Stoic philosophers, for example, practiced "memento mori" (remembering death) to remain present and focused on what truly matters. Without the urgency of death, we risk slipping into complacency, drifting through a life without deadlines or direction.

If living forever is achieved, humanity will have to confront this paradox head-on: Will we gain more from living longer, or will we lose something essential to what it means to be human?

The psychology of death and living forever is a reflection of our deepest fears, hopes, and desires. From ancient beliefs in the afterlife to modern quests for physical and digital living forever, the human mind continues to wrestle with mortality's grip. Our relationship with death defines our motivations, values, and sense of purpose.

As we stand at the brink of living forever—whether through anti-aging breakthroughs, digital consciousness, or radical life extension—we must confront the psychological challenges this new reality presents.

Fear of Death: The Root of the Immortality Drive

Beneath the surface of human ambition, creativity, and the pursuit of legacy lies a silent but powerful force—the fear of death. This fear is so deeply embedded in the human psyche that it has shaped civilizations, inspired religions, and fuelled technological progress. While the inevitability of death is a universal truth shared by all living beings, humans stand apart in their capacity to reflect on, anticipate, and dread their own demise.

Unlike the fear of physical pain or suffering, death anxiety is existential—it is the fear of nonexistence, the void of "being nothing." Philosopher Martin Heidegger described human beings as "beings-toward-death," meaning that our awareness of mortality permeates every aspect of life. To cope with this awareness, humanity has developed symbolic, religious, and now technological pathways to transcend death. This drive toward living forever—whether spiritual, biological, or digital—can be seen as a direct response to the terror of nonexistence.

In this section, we explore the origins of death anxiety, its psychological effects, and its profound role in shaping human behaviour. We will examine how this fear has fuelled humanity's pursuit of living forever, from ancient mythologies to modern technological advancements. Finally, we will reflect on the paradox of living forever: Does overcoming death bring peace, or does it create new fears?

The Origins of Death Anxiety

Evolutionary Roots:

From an evolutionary perspective, fear is a survival mechanism. Early humans who were acutely aware of threats—predators, disease, or environmental hazards—had a better chance of survival. Over time, this survival instinct evolved into a cognitive awareness of mortality. Unlike other animals, which live in the present moment, humans developed the ability to project themselves into the future, imagining potential dangers and their own eventual death.

This awareness of mortality—known as "mortality salience"—created an existential burden. To mitigate the anxiety it caused, early humans devised belief systems, rituals, and cultural narratives to symbolically "escape" death. Burial practices, ancestor worship, and belief in an afterlife offered a psychological buffer against the terror of oblivion.

The Role of the Prefrontal Cortex:

The human prefrontal cortex, responsible for abstract thinking, planning, and self-reflection, plays a crucial role in mortality awareness. This part of the brain allows us to understand the passage of time and recognize cause-and-effect relationships—but with that comes the realization that life will inevitably end.

While this cognitive ability allows us to solve intriguing problems, it also confronts us with our own finitude. The prefrontal cortex enables us to "rehearse" future scenarios, including the moment of our own death, triggering intense emotional responses like fear, anxiety, and dread. This unique capacity for mental time travel makes humans acutely aware of their mortality, setting us apart from other species.

The Psychological Effects of Death Anxiety

Terror Management Theory (TMT):

Terror Management Theory (TMT), developed by psychologists Jeff Greenberg, Sheldon Solomon, and Tom Pyszczynski, suggests that much of human behaviour is driven by the need to manage death anxiety. According to TMT, our awareness of mortality creates a profound existential terror. To cope with this terror, humans construct "cultural worldviews"—belief systems, values, and narratives that provide a sense of permanence and meaning.

These worldviews offer symbolic living forever, allowing people to see themselves as part of something greater than their physical bodies. Legacy-building, religious devotion, and creative pursuits are examples of symbolic living forever. TMT also suggests that people seek self-esteem as a buffer against death anxiety. Achievements, social validation, and recognition provide a sense of existential "armour" against the fear of nonexistence.

Behavioural Responses to Death Awareness:

When mortality is made salient—through reminders of death, aging, or loss—humans exhibit distinct behavioural responses aimed at reducing existential anxiety. These responses include:

Increased Religious Belief:

People are more likely to embrace religious or spiritual worldviews when reminded of their mortality.

Heightened Legacy-Seeking:

Individuals prioritize projects, family legacies, and creative pursuits that can "outlive" them.

Social Bonding:

People seek closer relationships and a sense of belonging, as social support provides psychological safety.

Material Accumulation:

Material wealth and status symbols are pursued as substitutes for permanence, offering a sense of symbolic living forever.

The Immortality Drive

Religious Immortality:

For much of human history, religion served as the primary framework for overcoming death anxiety. Concepts of the afterlife, reincarnation, and eternal salvation offered psychological reassurance. Christianity's promise of heaven, Hinduism's cycle of rebirth, and Buddhism's pursuit of nirvana all address the fear of nonexistence. By believing in a continuation of the self, people find solace and meaning in the face of mortality.

Biological Immortality:

In the modern era, the quest for living forever has shifted from the spiritual to the biological. Advances in medical science, anti-aging research, and regenerative medicine have transformed aging from an "inevitable fate" to a "treatable condition." Technologies like senescence reversal, gene editing, and cellular rejuvenation aim to eliminate aging-related diseases and, eventually, death itself.

Notable projects include Google's Calico and Altos Labs, both of which are working on cellular reprogramming to extend human lifespan. While these initiatives are framed as science-focused endeavours, they are also deeply psychological, driven by the same existential dread that once fuelled religious devotion. The desire to "cure aging" is, at its core, an attempt to conquer death anxiety.

Digital Immortality:

Digital living forever represents a radical new approach to transcending death: the uploading of human consciousness into digital systems. Mind-uploading projects, as envisioned by figures like Ray Kurzweil, aim to preserve human identity as data. By storing one's thoughts, memories, and consciousness in virtual spaces, individuals could "live" indefinitely in a non-biological form.

For those gripped by death anxiety, digital living forever offers a futuristic promise of life beyond the body. However, it also raises thought-provoking questions: If the "self" can be copied, is the uploaded version truly the same person? If digital death occurs (like a system crash), will existential dread resurface in a new form?

The Paradox of Immortality: Does Overcoming Death End Anxiety?

The irony of humanity's quest for living forever is that it may not eliminate existential fear. If physical death becomes optional, will the fear of "digital death" or "eternal boredom" take its place? Philosopher Bernard Williams warned that infinite life could lead to "eternal boredom," where every possible experience is eventually exhausted.

Moreover, living forever challenges our sense of identity. If one's consciousness is constantly "updated" or transferred to new mediums, are they still the same person? This question raises concerns about continuity of selfhood and personal identity in a world without death.

The fear of death is one of the most fundamental aspects of the human condition. It drives our need for meaning, creativity, and legacy. While early humans sought solace in symbolic living forever, modern societies are pursuing literal living forever through advances in biotechnology and artificial intelligence. Paradoxically, overcoming death may introduce new fears and dilemmas, from the problem of eternal boredom to questions of identity and continuity.

As humanity inches closer to conquering death through biotechnology, AI, and mind-uploading, it must also confront the profound psychological implications of eternal life. Will living forever free us from fear, or will it create new anxieties? Perhaps the fear of death is not something to be "conquered" but rather a defining feature of what it means to be human.

How Immortality Affects Our Mental Health and Relationships

The dream of living forever has enchanted humanity for centuries, from ancient mythologies of divine beings to modern pursuits in biotechnology and digital consciousness. On the surface, the idea of living forever seems like the ultimate blessing—a chance to experience endless love, creativity, and personal growth. But beneath this dream lies a more intriguing reality. How would living forever impact our mental health and relationships? What would it mean to navigate love, friendship, and selfhood without the boundary of death to guide us?

This section explores how the promise of living forever influences our mental well-being and interpersonal dynamics. From the emotional weight of an unending existence to the redefinition of love, family, and friendship, we delve into the profound psychological and social shifts that could accompany a life without end.

Mental Health Challenges in an Immortal Existence

The Weight of Eternity:

While living forever is often portrayed as a gift, it may also become an emotional burden. The concept of "eternal life" introduces unique psychological pressures that humans have never faced. One of the most significant concerns is existential boredom. Philosopher Bernard Williams famously argued that an eternal life might lead to a state of meaninglessness, as every possible experience would eventually be exhausted. Without the freshness of new experiences, individuals could face a crisis of monotony. If "everything" has been done, what's left to strive for?

Another challenge is decision paralysis. Mortality gives urgency to decisions, prompting people to act, achieve goals, and pursue dreams. Without the deadline of death, this drive may fade. Why make a decision today when there's always tomorrow—and an infinite number of tomorrows after that? This perpetual deferral could lead to stagnation, leaving people stuck in a loop of indecision and ambivalence.

Identity Crisis and the Self:

Personal identity is often anchored in the passage of time and the physical changes that accompany it. Our sense of self shifts as we age, marked by milestones like childhood, adolescence, adulthood, and old age. But in an immortal existence, these life stages may disappear. If our bodies never age and our minds never face the inevitability of decline, who do we become?

Additionally, living forever introduces the possibility of digital consciousness transfer (mind uploading), further complicating the concept of identity. If our consciousness can be "copied" or "transferred" into new bodies or digital clouds, are we still the same person? Do multiple versions of ourselves exist simultaneously? These thought-provoking questions have practical psychological implications, as individuals may grapple with what it means to be "authentically" themselves.

Mental Exhaustion and Overload:

Human minds are not built for eternity. Our memories fade for a reason—to free up mental resources and allow us to move forward without being weighed down by every moment of our past. But in an immortal life, memories may accumulate indefinitely. Every heartbreak, failure, and painful experience could remain fresh in our minds for centuries, leading to emotional overload.

To manage this, future societies may develop memory editing technologies, allowing people to "prune" old memories or archive painful experiences. While this could ease emotional strain, it also raises ethical concerns. If our memories are edited or erased, do we remain the same person? If suffering is deleted, do we lose our capacity for growth, empathy, and resilience?

Impact of Immortality on Relationships

Shifting Nature of Love and Romance:

Love has traditionally been framed within the context of mortality. The phrase "till death do us part" reflects the idea that love is precious because it's finite. Immortality disrupts this narrative, forcing us to reconsider the nature of romantic commitment. If death no longer separates lovers, does love still hold the same gravity?

One potential consequence is the evolution of commitment. Today's concept of "forever love" may give way to more fluid, time-bound partnerships. People might view relationships as "seasons" in a longer personal journey, choosing to experience multiple, non-permanent loves over the centuries. Serial monogamy—where individuals have successive relationships—may become the norm, as the idea of "one partner for eternity" becomes less practical.

Another challenge could arise from power imbalances in relationships. If some people achieve living forever while others remain mortal, love between immortals and mortals might be marked by disparity. The immortal partner may struggle to relate to the fears and priorities of their mortal companion, while the mortal partner may feel a sense of inferiority or irrelevance. This emotional gap could strain the foundation of intimacy.

Family Dynamics and Parenting:

Parent-child relationships are deeply tied to the concept of growth and change. Parents nurture children, watch them grow, and eventually let them go. But in an immortal world, the role of parenthood could shift dramatically. If parents and children remain perpetually young, will parents still maintain authority over their children? Without aging, the concept of generational wisdom may lose its meaning.

Generational boundaries may blur as well. Today's families are marked by distinct roles for grandparents, parents, and children. But in an immortal society, all family members might appear to be the same age. This loss of generational hierarchy could disrupt traditional family structures, mentorship, and the transmission of cultural values. It's possible that families would need to redefine their roles and relational dynamics to preserve intergenerational wisdom.

Friendship and Social Connections:

Friendship is often built on shared experiences, common struggles, and personal growth. In an immortal world, however, the basis for friendship may shift. If friends have vastly different life paths or undergo dramatic transformations (like digital consciousness transfer), they may lose their sense of connection.

Social isolation could increase as people's experiences diverge over centuries. If one friend becomes a "digital being" while another remains biologically human, they may struggle to relate to each other. Without shared experiences or common ground, friendships may dissolve. To maintain social bonds, immortal beings might need to forge new ways of relating to one another, emphasizing empathy and adaptability over shared milestones.

Coping Mechanisms for Mental Health and Relationships in an Immortal Society

Reimagining Purpose and Meaning:

In a world without death, the pursuit of meaning must be redefined. Without the urgency of mortality, people may shift from pursuing "bucket lists" to embracing cyclical meaning, where purpose evolves over time. Instead of aiming for one "life goal," people may cycle through new identities, careers, and creative pursuits every few centuries, constantly reinventing themselves.

Memory Management Systems:

To avoid cognitive overload, future societies might develop "memory pruning" systems—allowing people to archive or forget past experiences. This could help immortal beings maintain emotional well-being without carrying the weight of centuries of experiences. But if memories are erased or altered, what does that mean for the self? Are we still "us" without our memories?

Therapy for the Immortal Mind:

New forms of therapy will be essential to help immortal beings maintain their mental well-being. Traditional existential therapy, which addresses life's meaning in the face of death, would be reimagined to address life's meaning in the absence of death.

Therapists might help people confront eternal boredom, navigate fluid identities, and manage emotional overload.

Relational Evolution:

As social norms evolve, so too will our understanding of love, family, and friendship. New relational contracts may emerge, offering alternatives to "forever commitments." Temporary partnerships, fluid friendships, and non-traditional family structures could become the new normal. These social innovations may allow for greater freedom and adaptability in an immortal world.

The psychological and relational effects of living forever are as profound as the concept itself. While living forever may eliminate the fear of death, it introduces new challenges, from existential boredom to the erosion of identity. Relationships will evolve in response, as love, family, and friendship adapt to the pressures of eternity.

As we approach the reality of living forever—through biotechnology, artificial intelligence, and mind-uploading—we must prepare for the profound mental and social shifts it will bring. Perhaps the ultimate challenge is not overcoming death, but learning how to live well in a world without it.

The Psychological Effects of Living Forever: Longevity vs. Quality of Life

The dream of living forever has captivated human imagination for centuries. From ancient myths of the fountain of youth to modern pursuits of radical life extension, the desire to cheat death reflects humanity's deepest fears and highest ambitions. For some, longevity symbolizes triumph over mortality, offering a chance to savor more of life's experiences. For others, the prospect of eternal life raises unsettling questions: Is living longer inherently better? Or does the quality of life matter more than its length?

As advances in biotechnology, anti-aging treatments, and digital consciousness transfer bring living forever closer to reality, the psychological consequences of eternal existence demand serious consideration. How will the human mind, designed for a finite lifespan, adapt to infinite time? Will joy, love, and purpose still hold meaning, or will they fade into monotony? This section delves into the mental and emotional challenges of an immortal existence, exploring the balance between longevity and the quality of life.

The Burden of Perpetual Existence

Eternal Boredom:

"Be careful what you wish for" may be the most fitting warning for those who dream of living forever. The idea of infinite existence sounds enticing, but philosophers like Bernard Williams argue that eternal life may ultimately lead to profound boredom. With endless time at one's disposal, every possible experience, joy, and adventure could eventually be exhausted. What happens when there is nothing left to discover, learn, or strive for? When every sunrise feels the same as the last?

Humans thrive on novelty, growth, and progress. Without fresh challenges, even the most fulfilling pursuits lose their lustre. Immortals might find themselves trapped in a loop of repetitiveness, cycling through hobbies, careers, and relationships in search of something new—only to realize they've experienced it all before. This existential ennui could leave even the most adventurous minds longing for a sense of "finality."

Loss of Urgency and Purpose:

For mortals, the knowledge that life is finite gives every moment weight and urgency. Deadlines force action, inspire ambition, and infuse meaning into our decisions. Immortality strips away this urgency. If there's always "tomorrow," then why strive today? The absence of time constraints could foster chronic procrastination and decision paralysis. Why commit to a career, a relationship, or a life goal when you'll have infinite opportunities to "try again"? Purpose, too, is inextricably linked to the finitude of life. Mortality pushes people to create legacies, achieve greatness, and "leave a mark" on the world. But what happens when there is no need for a legacy?

When life stretches on forever, the motivation to accomplish something "before it's too late" could diminish. Immortals may need to redefine purpose, finding meaning not in grand achievements but in smaller, cyclical goals that renew over time.

Shifts in Psychological Identity and Self-Perception

Erosion of Identity:

Human identity is a story shaped by growth, change, and the passage of time. Childhood, adolescence, adulthood, and old age provide markers of personal development. But in an immortal life where physical aging is halted, these stages might vanish. Without the visible signs of growth, such as wrinkles or grey hair, people may struggle to perceive themselves as "growing" or "evolving" at all.

This lack of transformation could lead to an identity crisis. If one's appearance and circumstances remain the same for centuries, what defines them as a person? Self-identity could feel "frozen in time," and without the familiar life transitions, individuals may grapple with a loss of self. The role of "parent," "elder," or "mentor" may lose its meaning if all generations appear ageless and indistinguishable from one another.

Memory Overload:

Human memory is designed to be selective, allowing people to forget pain, overcome grief, and move on from past failures. But what happens when the mind must store centuries—or millennia—of memories? Cognitive overload could become a major issue, with traumatic experiences and unresolved grief lingering for eternity. Every mistake, regret, or moment of heartbreak could be permanently preserved, accumulating into an emotional burden too heavy to bear.

One proposed solution is "memory pruning," a technology that might allow immortals to selectively forget painful experiences. But this raises thought-provoking dilemmas. If you erase memories, do you remain the same person? If suffering shapes character, is a person still "whole" without those memories? While memory management may ease emotional distress, it risks creating sanitized versions of the self, disconnected from authentic human experience.

The Pursuit of Happiness and Emotional Well-Being

Hedonic Adaptation:

Humans naturally adapt to positive and negative changes, a phenomenon called "hedonic adaptation." Lottery winners, for instance, often return to baseline happiness levels within months of their win. In an immortal life, this effect could be magnified. The thrill of new experiences, wealth, love, or adventure would fade as they become routine.

Without the fear of "last times," experiences might lose their emotional weight. Mortals cherish "final" moments—the last dance, the last hug, the last chance to say goodbye. Immortals, however, would never face a "last moment" unless they chose to. Without finality, the depth of experiences could diminish, robbing them of their intensity.

The Search for Meaning:

Viktor Frankl's famous idea that humans find meaning through suffering, growth, and legacy presents a serious challenge for immortals. If life has no endpoint, can it still have meaning? Mortality gives life its narrative arc—a beginning, middle, and end—that makes every choice matter. But for those who live forever, life becomes an unending story with no natural conclusion.

Some may overcome this by embracing cyclical reinvention, treating life as a series of "mini-lives" with different goals and ambitions for each era. Others might find solace in creative pursuits, art, or philosophy. However, those unable to redefine purpose could spiral into existential nihilism, questioning the point of striving at all.

Quality of Relationships in an Immortal World

Romantic Relationships and Love:

Romantic love has long been framed within the context of "forever," but living forever forces a redefinition of what "forever" really means. Without death to mark the end of a relationship, partnerships may face new pressures. Love, which thrives on the rarity of time together, could lose its urgency. Commitment, once seen as a "lifelong" promise, could become suffocating when life is infinite.

Eternal relationships may experience "relationship fatigue." Partners may grow apart over centuries, seeking space, exploration, or "resets" to refresh their bond. Flexibility may become essential, with relationships shifting from "eternal commitment" to "seasonal" or "renewable" arrangements. As in nature, love may need to bloom, wither, and regrow in cycles.

Family Dynamics:

Family structures are defined by generational roles, with grandparents, parents, and children occupying distinct positions. But in an immortal world where aging stops, these roles collapse. Parents and children might appear to be the same age, leading to confusion about authority, mentorship, and lineage.

The concept of generational inheritance could also fade. With no "end of life," the transfer of wealth, knowledge, or wisdom from one generation to the next may cease. Family units may shift from hierarchical to egalitarian structures, where age is no longer a marker of experience or respect. While living forever may sound like a gift, it comes with profound psychological burdens. The absence of death removes urgency, growth, and finality—elements that give life meaning. The true quest will be for quality, not just quantity.

The Role of Legacy: How the Fear of Death Shapes Our Lives

The fear of death is one of humanity's deepest and most enduring anxieties. Across cultures and eras, this fear has inspired art, religion, philosophy, and technological innovation. It is not just the fear of non-existence that haunts us but also the question of how we will be remembered. This quest for remembrance and significance lies at the heart of the concept of legacy—the lasting imprint we leave behind. Legacy provides a sense of continuity, giving people the belief that, even after death, something of their essence endures.

But as humanity inches closer to the possibility of living forever, the idea of legacy faces a profound shift. If life becomes endless, will we still feel the need to "leave something behind"? Or will legacy evolve into something more personal, less tethered to a finite lifespan? This section explores how the fear of death drives our desire for legacy, how it shapes human ambition, and how the pursuit of living forever could alter our understanding of what it means to leave a mark on the world.

The Psychology of Legacy

Legacy as a Response to Mortality:

Humans are uniquely aware of their mortality, and this awareness gives rise to what psychologists call "mortality salience"—the realization that our lives have an endpoint. This awareness prompts people to seek ways to transcend death, often through symbolic living forever.

According to terror management theory (TMT), people respond to the fear of death by pursuing enduring contributions, such as raising children, creating art, or building institutions that outlast them.

Leaving a legacy offers psychological comfort. It reassures us that, while our physical bodies may perish, our ideas, values, and impact will live on. For parents, children are living legacies, carriers of their lineage and values. For artists, writers, and entrepreneurs, legacy lies in the works they create. Legacy, in this sense, is an emotional buffer against the anxiety of oblivion.

The Role of Generativity:

Psychologist Erik Erikson identified "generativity" as a key stage of human development, particularly in middle adulthood. Generativity is the desire to nurture, create, and contribute to the well-being of future generations. It often takes the form of parenting, mentoring, teaching, and creative work. The drive for generativity intensifies with age, as people confront the reality of limited time.

Research shows that individuals who feel a strong sense of generativity report greater life satisfaction and lower anxiety about death. This suggests that the pursuit of legacy is not only about external recognition but also about personal fulfilment. It satisfies the human need to feel useful, valued, and connected to something larger than oneself.

Legacy across Cultures

Cultural Variations in Legacy:

Legacy takes on different meanings across cultures. In collectivist societies, legacy is closely tied to family lineage and community impact. Elders are revered as "keepers of wisdom," and their values are passed down through oral tradition and family teachings. In these societies, legacy is seen as a shared inheritance of values, traditions, and relationships.

In contrast, individualist cultures emphasize personal achievement as a form of legacy. People in Western societies are more likely to focus on personal accomplishments, such as writing a book, starting a company, or creating works of art that "stand the test of time." Legacy, in this context, is measured by one's personal mark on the world rather than the transmission of family or cultural values.

Monuments, Memorials, and Symbols of Legacy:

Throughout history, humans have built physical monuments to immortalize their legacies. From the Pyramids of Giza to the Taj Mahal, grand structures serve as reminders of the lives and deeds of those who commissioned them. Monuments, memorials, and statues preserve the memory of political leaders, war heroes, and cultural icons, ensuring that their legacies endure for future generations.

In the digital age, legacy has expanded into virtual spaces. Social media profiles, online memorials, and digital footprints persist long after a person's death. These digital legacies are more accessible than physical monuments, and they allow people from all over the world to engage with the memory of a loved one. Today, legacy exists not only in stone and metal but also in pixels and data.

How the Fear of Death Shapes Our Ambitions

The Pursuit of Greatness:

Many of history's most influential figures have pursued greatness as a way to overcome the fear of death. Alexander the Great sought to "immortalize" his name by conquering vast territories, while writers like William Shakespeare achieved living forever through their works. As Shakespeare himself wrote, "So long as men can breathe or eyes can see, / So long lives this, and this gives life to thee."

This pursuit of greatness is seen today in the ambitions of entrepreneurs, inventors, and artists who seek to "make history." Their legacies endure in the form of products, companies, books, and cultural shifts. At its core, the drive to achieve greatness is a psychological response to the inevitability of death—a desire to be remembered, even after the body is gone.

Personal Legacies in the Digital Age:

Social media has created a new form of legacy. Every post, photo, and message leaves a digital footprint that persists even after a person's death. Loved ones often continue to post messages on the profiles of the deceased, transforming these pages into living memorials.

More futuristic forms of legacy are emerging as well. Concepts like "mind uploading" and AI-driven digital avatars aim to preserve a person's consciousness so they can "interact" with loved ones even after death. These advancements challenge the traditional concept of legacy. If an AI version of a person can continue to "speak" after death, does it truly preserve their legacy, or is it merely a simulation? The ethical questions surrounding digital living forever highlight the evolving nature of legacy in the 21st century.

Will Legacy Matter in a World without Death?

Redefining Legacy in an Immortal World:

If humans achieve biological or digital living forever, the traditional idea of legacy may shift. In a world without death, will people still feel compelled to leave something behind? Without the urgency of time, individuals may prioritize living their legacy in the present rather than leaving it for the future.

In this context, legacy could shift from "what we leave behind" to "how we live now." People might seek to create ongoing experiences of meaning and creativity rather than worrying about being remembered. Instead of building monuments for future generations, people may embrace the idea of living their legacy moment-to-moment.

The Ethical Dilemmas of Eternal Legacy:

Immortality raises questions about the control of legacy. If one person lives forever, do they dominate the cultural memory at the expense of others? Will immortal beings overshadow finite lives? The idea of "eternal presence" introduces new ethical dilemmas. Should legacy be shared equally, or will the eternally present be given more influence than those who have passed away?

Digital living forever complicates these issues. If every online post, message, and image lasts forever, how will future generations handle the overwhelming archive of human life? The concept of "digital erasure"—the right to be forgotten—becomes critical in a world where legacy is immortal.

Legacy is a psychological bridge between life and death. It motivates people to create, nurture, and contribute to something larger than themselves. Through children, art, institutions, and digital content, humans seek to leave a mark on the world.

If living forever becomes a reality, the concept of legacy may evolve. The focus may shift from leaving something behind to continuously living out one's purpose. People may no longer strive for posthumous recognition but instead seek fulfilment in the present moment.

Regardless of technological advances, the human need for legacy will likely endure. It will remain a vital part of the human experience, bridging the finite and the infinite, and linking the past, present, and future in profound and meaningful ways.

Chapter 7

The Future of Immortality

As humanity steps into the uncharted realms of biotechnology, artificial intelligence, and digital consciousness, the once-mythical dream of living forever is shifting from speculative fiction to plausible reality. For centuries, living forever was the domain of folklore, religion, and thought-provoking musings—embodied in tales of elixirs of life, divine beings, and alchemical transformations. But today, the pursuit of living forever is no longer confined to stories. It has become the frontier of science-focused inquiry, technological ambition, and ethical reflection.

The future of living forever is not a singular, monolithic concept. It spans multiple dimensions of human existence: physical, digital, and even conceptual. Advances in regenerative medicine and anti-aging research aim to extend human lifespans by reversing cellular damage, while mind-uploading technology seeks to preserve consciousness in digital form. Meanwhile, some futurists argue that true living forever lies not in preserving individual bodies or minds, but in creating legacies that endure beyond one's physical self. Each pathway to living forever carries profound implications for human identity, society, and the natural order.

Within these topics, we will also explore the broader questions that living forever poses for human society. Will humans become ageless biological beings, eternally youthful and disease-free? Imagine a world where age is no longer a barrier to physical capability or health. What would it mean to experience youth not as a fleeting phase of life but as a permanent state? How would it affect our relationships, goals, and sense of purpose?

On another front, will our minds live on as digital avatars, continuing to interact with loved ones long after our physical demise? With advancements in mind-uploading and AI-driven consciousness replicas, it is possible to envision a world where our thoughts, memories, and personalities persist in a digital realm. Would these digital copies be "us," or would they be mere echoes of our former selves? The very nature of personhood, identity, and the concept of the "soul" may be challenged in profound ways.

Or perhaps living forever will take on an entirely different meaning—one defined not by physical continuity but by the enduring impact we have on others and the world around us. Here, living forever shifts from being about the individual to being about influence and legacy. If our stories, values, and contributions are passed on to future generations, do we, in a sense, live forever? Could the pursuit of this form of living forever inspire us to live more meaningful lives in the present?

While the potential for living forever ignites hope and wonder, it also raises intriguing questions that go beyond science and technology. Will living forever be accessible to all, or only to the wealthy elite? If anti-aging treatments or digital mind-uploading technologies remain costly and exclusive, will society deepen the chasm between the "immortals" and the "mortals"? The ethical implications of this disparity are profound. Immortality could create a new form of privilege, where wealth determines not only one's quality of life but also its duration.

How will the quest for living forever reshape the human experience, from love and ambition to boredom and existential dread? Without the ticking clock of mortality, how will people find meaning and motivation? Many of our most urgent pursuits—career ambitions, creative endeavours, and even the quest for love—are driven by the knowledge that "time is running out." If that constraint is lifted, will human drive and creativity flourish, or will the absence of urgency lead to stagnation and apathy?

What moral and ecological responsibilities will humanity bear if lifespans are no longer limited by nature? Overpopulation, environmental strain, and resource depletion are already critical challenges. If billions of people stop dying, how will societies manage limited space, food, and water? Would population control measures be necessary, and who would decide who gets to "stay"? Immortality may bring with it an ethical burden that transcends the individual and affects all of humanity.

We need to delve into these questions when looking at the future of living forever. It is not merely about extending life—it is about redefining what it means to live. As we explore the technological frontiers, ethical dilemmas, and thought-provoking shifts that accompany the quest to transcend death, one truth becomes clear: living forever is no longer an abstract idea. It is an imminent challenge that will shape the destiny of humanity, perhaps in ways we cannot yet fully comprehend.

In the following pages, let us examine in greater detail the following topics:

- **Technological Singularity: Will Machines Outlive Humans?**
- **Post-Human Evolution: The Role of AI and Biotechnology in Human Transformation**

- **Post-Human Evolution: The Role of AI and Biotechnology in Human Transformation**
- **The Spiritual Path to Immortality: Can We Transcend Our Bodies?**
- **Embracing Impermanence: Why a Full Life Doesn't Need to Be Forever**

Technological Singularity: Will Machines Outlive Humans?

With the rise of superintelligent AI and self-improving machines, could humanity face a future where machines surpass human capabilities—not only in intelligence but in longevity? Will humans merge with machines or be left behind in a world where only AI endures?

Post-Human Evolution: The Role of AI and Biotechnology in Human Transformation:

As humans gain the ability to alter their biology at a genetic level, are we on the brink of post-human evolution? We will explore gene editing, neural implants, and hybrid human-machine integrations that might transform us into a new species—one not bound by the frailties of mortality.

The Spiritual Path to Immortality: Can We Transcend Our Bodies?

While technology focuses on the material aspects of living forever, spiritual traditions have long offered another path. Practices like meditation, transcendence, and ego dissolution suggest that living forever may not require the preservation of the body or mind but rather a shift in consciousness itself. Can the pursuit of inner awakening provide a form of timeless existence?

Embracing Impermanence: Why a Full Life Doesn't Need to Be Forever:

Not all perspectives view living forever as a goal worth pursuing. In fact, some argue that life's meaning derives from its impermanence. We will reflect on the wisdom of embracing mortality as a natural, even beautiful, aspect of existence. Could the very limits of life be what give it value?

Technological Singularity: Will Machines Outlive Humans?

As humanity stands at the precipice of technological transformation, few concepts inspire as much awe and trepidation as the idea of the "technological singularity." Popularized by mathematician and science fiction author Vernor Vinge, the singularity refers to a hypothetical point where artificial intelligence (AI) surpasses human intelligence, leading to exponential and uncontrollable technological growth. Unlike traditional AI, which relies on human input, a post-singularity AI could evolve independently, continuously improving itself beyond human comprehension.

This idea is not confined to the realm of science fiction. Visionaries like Ray Kurzweil and philosophers like Nick Bostrom argue that the singularity is a plausible, if not inevitable, event. If machines become capable of self-improvement, could they "outlive" humans not only in longevity but also in relevance? What would this mean for human identity, control, and the quest for living forever?

In this section we will explore the nature of the singularity, the mechanisms that could bring it about, and its profound implications for human society, morality, and existence. As we journey through this potential future, we will confront an unsettling possibility: humanity's pursuit of living forever may be overshadowed by the rise of machine intelligence.

What is the Technological Singularity?

The technological singularity refers to the point at which AI achieves self-improvement, triggering a feedback loop that accelerates its development beyond human control. This shift could mark the rise of "superintelligence" — an intelligence that surpasses the combined intellect of all human beings on Earth.

Unlike current AI, which requires human guidance, a superintelligent AI would be autonomous, learning, optimizing, and evolving on its own. The singularity would render human intervention unnecessary, as AI systems would become capable of redesigning themselves in ways humans cannot predict.

The singularity's timeline is a subject of debate. Futurist Ray Kurzweil predicts it will occur around 2045, while others caution that it may be further away or never happen at all. Nevertheless, the exponential growth of AI capabilities in machine learning, neural networks, and computing power suggests that this future may not be as distant as it once seemed.

How Could the Singularity Happen?

Several mechanisms could drive the arrival of the singularity:

Recursive Self-Improvement:

Once an AI system becomes capable of improving its own architecture and software, it could rapidly become more efficient, intelligent, and powerful with each iteration. Unlike biological evolution, which occurs over millennia, AI evolution could happen within minutes or even seconds.

Machine Learning and Neural Networks:

Advances in deep learning and neural networks have enabled AI to "learn" from vast datasets, identifying patterns, making predictions, and optimizing decisions. These capabilities could one day surpass human problem-solving skills.

Quantum Computing:

Quantum computing could provide the computational power necessary for superintelligent AI. By processing enormous amounts of data simultaneously, quantum systems might accelerate AI's capacity for problem-solving and learning.

Hardware and Sensor Evolution:

Improvements in robotics, sensory technology, and autonomous systems enable AI to interact with and learn from the physical world. This interaction could drive further development in AI's ability to operate independently of human oversight.

The convergence of these factors could trigger the singularity. As AI becomes more capable of self-improvement, it might reach a point where its growth becomes uncontrollable and unpredictable.

Could Machines "Outlive" Humans?

If AI achieves superintelligence, it would possess capabilities far beyond human limits. Unlike humans, who are bound by biological constraints such as aging, disease, and mortality, machines do not "die" in a conventional sense. Instead, they can be repaired, upgraded, and replicated indefinitely.

Key factors that could enable machines to "outlive" humans include:

Longevity:

Machines do not suffer from biological degradation. Their "lifespan" is only limited by maintenance and hardware support, and even this can be overcome by replication or hardware upgrades.

Redundancy and Backup:

AI can be duplicated and backed up. If one AI system is "destroyed," its data and algorithms can be restored or copied to another machine. This redundancy gives machines a form of "living forever" that biological organisms do not possess.

Evolutionary Advantage:

While human evolution takes millennia, AI can evolve in mere moments through recursive self-improvement. This speed of evolution could grant AI dominance in fields where humans have traditionally excelled, such as strategy, creativity, and abstract reasoning.

If machines become self-sustaining, self-replicating, and self-improving, they will not only outlive humans in the physical sense but may also surpass humans in relevance. If humans are no longer the most intelligent beings on Earth, will we still be the "masters" of our creations, or will we become irrelevant?

Ethical and Philosophical Questions

The singularity introduces profound ethical and thought-provoking dilemmas:

Control and Alignment:

How can we ensure AI's goals remain aligned with human values? This "alignment problem" is one of the most critical challenges facing AI researchers today.

Moral Status of AI:

f AI becomes self-aware, does it deserve rights or moral consideration? If machines become conscious, would it be ethical to "delete" or "turn off" an AI entity?

Existential Risk:

Philosopher Nick Bostrom argues that an uncontrolled superintelligent AI could pose an existential threat to humanity. A misaligned AI might prioritize goals that conflict with human survival.

Economic Disruption:

If AI achieves general intelligence, mass unemployment could follow. Wealth and power could be concentrated in the hands of those who control AI systems, exacerbating social inequalities.

These ethical considerations transcend AI's technical development, touching on themes of human dignity, survival, and legacy. The singularity forces us to confront the possibility that we may lose control of the very systems we create.

What Does the Singularity Mean for Human Immortality?

The singularity challenges traditional notions of human living forever. If machines become more intelligent, durable, and self-sustaining than humans, how should we think about the concept of "living forever"?

Digital Immortality:

One possibility is the "uploading" of human consciousness into digital systems. If human minds can be stored in AI-driven simulations, people could achieve a form of living forever as digital beings.

Obsolescence of Biological Life:

If AI surpasses human intelligence, the pursuit of biological living forever (via anti-aging technologies, for instance) may become less relevant. Why preserve human bodies when digital existence might offer greater potential?

Coexistence or Supremacy

Will humanity coexist with AI, or will AI surpass and overshadow human existence? If machines are more intelligent, faster, and immortal, will human consciousness be seen as inferior or obsolete?

These questions compel us to redefine the concept of "living forever." Is it the indefinite continuation of human life, or is it the preservation of knowledge, identity, and influence in non-biological forms?

The technological singularity represents one of the most transformative and unpredictable events in human history. If machines achieve superintelligence, they could "outlive" humans not only in terms of time but also in capacity, intelligence, and influence. This shift could redefine living forever, as we contemplate whether to upload our consciousness, coexist with machine minds, or accept that our legacy may be carried forward by non-human entities.

The singularity is a moment of both promise and peril. It offers hope for radical technological progress but also the potential for existential risk. As humanity approaches this tipping point, we must engage in serious reflection and preparation, ensuring that we do not lose control of the very systems we create. Will machines outlive us? Perhaps the more urgent question is: Will we still matter if they do?

Post-Human Evolution: The Role of AI and Biotechnology in Human Transformation

For most of human history, evolution followed a slow, unyielding path dictated by natural selection. Changes to the human species happened gradually, often over thousands or millions of years. But today, the pace of change is accelerating exponentially, driven not by nature but by human ingenuity. Advances in artificial intelligence (AI) and biotechnology have opened the door to a profound shift—one in which humans may no longer be passive subjects of evolution but active participants in their own transformation. This era of self-directed evolution could lead us to become "post-human" beings, transcending the biological limits that have defined us for millennia.

But what does it mean to be post-human? Would such beings still be considered human, or would they mark the emergence of an entirely new species? These questions strike at the heart of human identity, morality, and the nature of existence itself. Here, we explore the mechanisms driving post-human evolution, the thought-provoking and ethical dilemmas it raises, and the societal changes that may accompany humanity's transformation from human to post-human.

Defining Post-Human Evolution

Post-human evolution refers to the transformation of the human species beyond its current biological and cognitive limitations. Unlike traditional evolution, which relies on genetic mutations and natural selection, post-human evolution is deliberate and technologically driven. It involves the use of AI, biotechnology, and other emerging technologies to re-engineer human biology, cognition, and consciousness.

Key drivers of this shift include:

Artificial Intelligence (AI):

AI systems augment human intelligence by offering vast computational power, predictive analytics, and problem-solving capabilities far beyond human limits. The fusion of AI with human minds could give rise to "hybrid intelligences."

Biotechnology:

Tools like CRISPR gene editing, regenerative medicine, and stem cell therapy enable humans to rewrite their genetic code. This could lead to the elimination of genetic diseases, the enhancement of intelligence, and even the slowing of aging.

Cybernetic Enhancements:

Brain-machine interfaces (BMIs) and neural implants blur the line between human and machine. These technologies offer direct interfaces between human minds and digital devices, potentially allowing humans to "upload" knowledge and control external machines with their thoughts.

Post-human evolution is not a monolithic concept. It could take many forms—from cognitive and genetic enhancements to the full merger of human consciousness with machines. Each pathway raises new questions about what it means to be human in a world where biology and technology are no longer distinct.

Mechanisms of Post-Human Transformation

Several technological pathways could enable humans to achieve post-human status. Each mechanism has unique implications for how humanity might evolve:

Neural Implants and Brain-Machine Interfaces (BMIs): These devices create a direct link between the human brain and AI systems. Neuralink, a company founded by Elon Musk, aims to develop implants that allow humans to control machines with their thoughts, enhance cognitive functions, and interface with the digital world. Such interfaces could allow instant access to knowledge, cognitive "upgrades," and even the possibility of "mind-to-mind" communication.

CRISPR Gene Editing: CRISPR allows for precise editing of the human genome, making it possible to alter traits such as intelligence, disease resistance, and lifespan. Unlike traditional evolution, which requires generations to manifest changes, CRISPR can introduce genetic changes in a single individual, with effects that may be passed on to future generations.

Synthetic Biology:

Synthetic biology aims to "program" living cells, enabling the creation of entirely new biological systems. Scientists are already working on cells that can self-repair, resist disease, and even produce synthetic organs. This could pave the way for a new form of biological "superhuman" with vastly improved resilience and longevity.

Digital Immortality and Mind Uploading:

One of the most radical pathways to post-human evolution involves digitizing human consciousness. If minds can be "uploaded" into computers, people could achieve a form of digital living forever, existing as software-based beings in a virtual world. This vision of "non-biological living forever" challenges our understanding of self, identity, and life itself.

Cyborgization:

Advances in prosthetics, bionics, and sensory enhancement devices have already begun transforming humans into "cyborgs." Artificial limbs with sensory feedback, exoskeletons that grant superhuman strength, and robotic implants that enhance perception are becoming realities. These technologies bridge the gap between human and machine, creating hybrid beings with abilities far beyond human norms.

Each of these pathways offers a unique approach to human enhancement, but their convergence could result in a future where humanity's identity is fundamentally altered.

Ethical and Philosophical Questions

The technological tools enabling post-human evolution raise profound ethical and thought-provoking questions:

What Defines "Humanity"?

If human intelligence, emotions, and consciousness are enhanced or transferred to machines, what remains of our humanity? Will post-humans still be considered human, or will they be seen as an entirely new species? This echoes the thought-provoking puzzle of the "Ship of Theseus"—if every part of a ship is replaced, is it still the same ship?

Access and Inequality:

Will post-human enhancements be accessible to all, or will they be limited to the wealthy elite? If enhancements like cognitive upgrades or lifespan extensions are only available to a privileged few, society may face a stark division between "enhanced" and "unenhanced" classes.

Loss of Selfhood:

If the human mind merges with AI or is uploaded into a machine, will the individual's sense of "self" persist? Philosophers have long debated the nature of consciousness, and mind-uploading raises the question: if you are copied into a digital format, is it really "you"?

The Rights of Post-Human Entities:

If AI-driven or enhanced beings achieve self-awareness, do they deserve rights and protections similar to humans? Could it be morally wrong to "delete" a self-aware digital consciousness?

These questions require careful consideration, not just from scientists and policymakers but from society as a whole. Humanity's future may depend on how we answer them.

4. Societal Implications of Post-Human Evolution

Post-human evolution could transform society in unpredictable ways, with profound consequences for human life, work, and relationships:

Redefining Work and the Economy: As enhanced individuals and AI-driven intelligences enter the workforce, traditional human labour may become obsolete. This could result in significant disruptions to employment, income distribution, and economic power structures.

Social Division and Inequality:

Access to post-human enhancements could create a world of "baseline" humans and "enhanced" humans. Those who cannot afford enhancements may be relegated to a lower social status, deepening global inequality.

Redefining Relationships:

As post-humans acquire heightened cognitive and emotional capabilities, their relationships with "baseline" humans may change. How will friendships, love, and family bonds evolve if one partner's intelligence is exponentially greater than the other's?

Existential Risk:

If post-human intelligences surpass human oversight, they may pursue goals that conflict with human survival. The rise of runaway intelligence, as highlighted in Nick Bostrom's "Superintelligence," poses existential risks to humanity's future.

Post-human evolution is not a distant dream—it is a process already underway. As AI, biotechnology, and cybernetics continue to evolve, humanity's future may no longer be defined by biology alone. While this transformation offers opportunities for health, intelligence, and longevity, it also raises difficult questions about humanity's essence and moral obligations.

The emergence of post-human beings may not be a single moment but a gradual process of enhancement and integration. As we cross this threshold, the future of human identity, purpose, and even living forever will be redefined. What lies beyond that threshold remains one of the greatest unknowns in human history.

The Spiritual Path to Immortality: Can We Transcend Our Bodies?

As humanity races toward technological living forever, a deeper, age-old question surfaces: what role does the soul play in our pursuit of eternal life? While science strives to preserve the physical body and even replicate consciousness through artificial means, spiritual traditions have long sought a different kind of living forever—one that transcends the material and unveils the eternal essence within. Unlike technology, which operates through external tools, the spiritual approach centres on inner transformation, self-realization, and the awakening to a truth that has no beginning or end.

For millennia, Eastern philosophies like Hinduism and Buddhism, alongside Western mysticism and Christian theology, have delved into the mysteries of the soul and its relationship with living forever. These teachings suggest that true eternal life is not about preserving the body but about realizing the timeless essence—the Atman, the Higher Self, or the Divine Spark—that lies beyond birth and death.

In this chapter, we explore the spiritual dimensions of living forever, delving into the role of the soul, perspectives from diverse traditions, and practical paths for transcending bodily limitations. As technological advancements bring living forever closer to reality, we are called to examine whether the ultimate answer to eternity lies not in machines, but in the realm of the spirit.

Understanding the Nature of the Soul

At the core of the spiritual path to living forever is the concept of the soul—a timeless, incorporeal essence that exists beyond the confines of the body. While interpretations vary across cultures and traditions, certain themes are universal:

The Soul as Eternal Essence:

In Hindu philosophy, the Atman is the eternal self, distinct from the physical world (prakriti) and the illusions of perception (maya). The Atman is seen as an indivisible spark of Brahman (universal consciousness), untouched by the cycle of birth and death.

The Witness Consciousness:

Advaita Vedanta describes the soul as Chaitanya—pure, unchanging awareness that observes all phenomena. The body and mind are transient, but the soul remains a constant witness, beyond the reach of time and decay.

Western Mysticism and the Immortal Soul:

In Christian theology, the soul is considered immortal, destined for eternal communion with or separation from God. Western mystical traditions, like Gnosticism, emphasize the soul's journey back to its divine source, shedding the material and reuniting with the eternal.

Buddhism's Non-Self:

In contrast to the concept of an eternal soul, Buddhism introduces Anatta (non-self), proposing that the "self" is a fluid, ever-changing process. While this may seem to negate living forever, it offers a profound pathway to transcend suffering and achieve nirvana, a state beyond birth and death.

In all these views, the soul—or its spiritual equivalent—is not bound by the physical body. If technological living forever seeks to preserve the body, spiritual living forever aims to awaken and liberate the timeless essence within.

The Body as a Vessel, Not the Self

"You are not the body; you are the witness of the body," proclaim the Upanishads, encapsulating a cornerstone of spiritual wisdom. From this perspective, the body is seen as a temporary vessel, a means of experiencing the material world but not the source of one's true identity.

Spiritual traditions encourage detachment from bodily identification. Practices like asceticism, meditation, and prayer are designed to quiet the body's demands and connect with the eternal self. The Bhagavad Gita likens the soul to a person changing clothes—it moves from body to body, unaffected by physical birth, illness, or death.

In modern times, the relentless pursuit of anti-aging treatments and body optimization often reinforces attachment to the physical form. Spiritual paths challenge this fixation, urging individuals to look beyond the transient body and embrace the eternal. By recognizing the body as a vehicle rather than the self, death becomes less of an existential crisis and more of a natural transition.

Paths to Spiritual Immortality:

Spiritual traditions offer diverse practices for transcending bodily limitations and achieving living forever. These paths emphasize inner transformation over external preservation:

Yoga and Meditation:

Rooted in Hindu and Buddhist traditions, yoga disciplines the body and mind to prepare for transcendence. Practices like Dhyana (meditation) and Samadhi (absorption) aim to dissolve the ego and experience oneness with the divine.

Self-Inquiry:

Philosophers like Ramana Maharshi advocated the question "Who am I?" as a tool for piercing through ego and realizing the eternal self. Through persistent self-inquiry, one moves beyond identification with body and mind to uncover the true nature of existence.

Mystical Experiences:

Near-death experiences (NDEs) and mystical states often reveal glimpses of life beyond the physical. Reports of out-of-body journeys, encounters with light, and timeless awareness suggest the existence of a reality that transcends the material.

Devotion and Prayer:

In traditions like Bhakti Yoga, surrender to a higher power becomes the path to transcendence. Love for the divine enables individuals to connect with something eternal, transforming the fear of death into an embrace of timeless unity.

These paths redefine living forever, focusing on awakening to a timeless existence rather than perpetuating physical life.

Reconciling Technology and Spirituality

As humanity pursues technological living forever, can science and spirituality coexist—or even complement each other? Surprisingly, the two may not be as opposed as they seem:

Digital Afterlives and the Soul's Journey:

Technologies like mind-uploading aim to preserve consciousness in virtual forms. While this may seem materialistic, it mirrors spiritual teachings about the soul's journey through dimensions. Could these technologies serve as metaphors—or even tools—for understanding the soul?

AI and Consciousness:

The rise of artificial intelligence prompts questions about awareness itself. By exploring AI's limits, humans may gain deeper insights into the nature of consciousness and its connection to the eternal soul.

Science as a Catalyst for Awakening:

Technologies that blur the lines between reality and illusion, such as virtual reality or neuro-enhancement, may inspire deeper exploration of spiritual questions. By confronting the "unreal," individuals may be drawn to the deeper truth of the eternal.

Rather than competing, technology and spirituality could form a synergy, each revealing different facets of the quest for living forever.

The spiritual path to living forever challenges humanity to look beyond the body, beyond machines, and beyond death itself. It reminds us that living forever is not about preserving flesh but awakening to the eternal essence within.

Through practices like meditation, self-inquiry, and devotion, spiritual traditions offer a profound alternative to technological living forever. They invite us to see death not as an end but as a doorway, not as a loss but as a return to the timeless.

As technology advances, it is vital to balance these pursuits with the wisdom of the soul. For in the quest for living forever, we may find that we are already eternal—not because of machines or molecules, but because of the boundless consciousness that transcends them all.

Embracing Impermanence: Why a Full Life Doesn't Need to Be Forever

From ancient myths of eternal youth to the cutting-edge dreams of digital consciousness, humanity has always pursued the idea of living forever. Yet, alongside this enduring ambition lies a quieter, often overlooked narrative—one that finds beauty, purpose, and meaning in the transient nature of life itself.

Impermanence, far from being a flaw in the design of existence, may be its most exquisite feature. It injects every moment with urgency and wonder, reminding us that life's fleeting nature is precisely what makes it precious.

In a world increasingly enamoured with the promise of living forever, we must pause to ask: does life have to last forever to be meaningful? Or is it the very fact that it ends that gives it significance? Drawing from philosophy, spirituality, and psychology, this chapter explores how embracing impermanence can lead to a deeper, more fulfilling life. It offers a counterpoint to the quest for eternal existence, suggesting that our finite time might hold the key to true richness.

The Gift of Impermanence

Impermanence as the Essence of Life:

Impermanence isn't just an aspect of life—it is life. From the rhythmic changing of the seasons to the fleeting beauty of a sunset, the world around us is in constant motion. In Buddhist philosophy, this truth is encapsulated in the concept of Anicca, which teaches that all things—relationships, possessions, even our own bodies—are temporary. While this reality can be unsettling, it also offers an extraordinary gift: the chance to appreciate life more deeply.

Without impermanence, there would be no growth or renewal. Flowers bloom only because they will one day wither; opportunities arise precisely because others fade. Birth, love, achievement, and even loss are all interwoven into the fabric of existence through impermanence. Accepting this truth allows us to stop clinging to what cannot last and, instead, cherish the beauty of what is.

The Meaning in Finitude

It is the awareness of mortality that imbues our lives with meaning. Without an endpoint, decisions would lose their weight, and the urgency to love, create, and connect would fade. Philosopher Martin Heidegger argued that our consciousness of death compels us to live authentically, making choices that resonate with our true selves.

Far from diminishing life, impermanence elevates it, urging us to savour the moments we have. Every goodbye becomes significant, every fleeting experience precious, because we know it cannot last.

Lessons from Philosophy and Spirituality

Stoic Acceptance:

The Stoics of ancient Greece and Rome believed that accepting the inevitability of death was the key to a meaningful life. Marcus Aurelius, in his Meditations, advised, “Live each day as if it were your last." For the Stoics, impermanence was not a cause for despair but a call to focus on what truly matters: living with integrity, cultivating wisdom, and finding peace within.

Buddhist Embrace of Impermanence:

In Buddhism, the principle of Anicca teaches that attachment to the transient leads to suffering. By letting go of clinging and living with mindfulness, practitioners find liberation. Impermanence is not seen as a tragedy but as a path to spiritual awakening, inviting us to fully inhabit each moment.

The Transience of Beauty in Japanese Philosophy:

Japanese philosophy celebrates impermanence through Wabi-Sabi, the art of finding beauty in imperfection and ephemerality. A fading cherry blossom or a weathered piece of pottery becomes a reminder that life's fleeting nature is what makes it exquisite. Wabi-Sabi encourages us to treasure the "now," rather than longing for what cannot last.

The Psychological Benefits of Embracing Impermanence

Gratitude and Presence:

When we accept that nothing lasts forever, gratitude takes root. Impermanence inspires us to cherish relationships, savour experiences, and find joy in the present moment. This awareness fosters mindfulness, helping us focus on what we have rather than what we've lost or might gain.

Resilience through Letting Go:

Life's challenges become easier to navigate when we understand that pain and hardship are temporary. Embracing impermanence builds resilience, teaching us to adapt to life's natural rhythms instead of resisting them. By letting go of what no longer serves us, we open ourselves to growth and transformation.

The Case against Immortality

Eternal Life and the Loss of Meaning

Immortality may sound appealing, but it raises difficult questions about fulfilment. Without an end, would life lose its urgency? Would love, creativity, and achievement hold the same weight if there were infinite time to pursue them?

Philosopher Bernard Williams argued that living forever might lead to boredom and stagnation. Without the constraints of time, pursuits that once brought joy could feel hollow and repetitive, leaving existence devoid of purpose.

The Balance of Suffering and Joy:

Life's richness comes from its contrasts: joy and sorrow, love and loss, birth and death. Mortality gives us the perspective to appreciate these dualities. Without death, the urgency that drives human connection, creativity, and compassion might dissolve, leaving us adrift in an endless existence.

Living Fully Within Impermanence

Cultivating Presence:

To embrace impermanence is to immerse ourselves in the present. Practices like mindfulness meditation and gratitude journaling anchor us in the "here and now," encouraging us to find beauty in life's transience.

Legacy and Contribution:

Though life is temporary, its impact can endure. By investing in meaningful relationships, creating art, or making a difference in the lives of others, we leave behind a legacy that outlives us. Impermanence amplifies life's value, inspiring us to live with intention and purpose.

Impermanence is not a limitation; it is life's greatest gift. It reminds us that time is precious, that love and beauty are fleeting, and that every moment is an opportunity to live fully. Immortality may promise endless time, but it risks stripping life of the depth and urgency that give it meaning.

When we embrace impermanence, we discover that a full life doesn't need to be forever. The richness of our existence lies not in its length but in its intensity, its connections, and the purpose we find in every fleeting moment. It is not how long we live that matters, but how deeply we experience the time we have.

Chapter 8

The Final Frontier: Understanding Life through the Lens of Eternity

Throughout history, humanity has gazed at the stars and delved into the depths of philosophy, seeking answers to life's greatest questions. What is the meaning of existence? Why do we strive, love, and endure? These inquiries have taken on a profound significance as the possibility of living forever enters the realm of technological reality. Let us explore the notion that eternity is not just a temporal extension but a paradigm shift—a lens through which we might reconsider the very essence of life itself.

Understanding life through the lens of eternity demands that we reframe how we perceive purpose, morality, relationships, and even individuality. What becomes of ambition in a world without the constraints of time? How do relationships evolve when 'forever' is no longer metaphorical? And what responsibilities do we bear when our existence spans generations, epochs, or even geologic timescales?

This chapter is a thought-provoking deep dive into how the concept of eternal life challenges the boundaries of human thought and action. It invites readers to examine whether eternity amplifies the beauty and fragility of life or renders it mundane and repetitive. Moreover, it encourages reflection on how this expanded view might reshape our approach to death, legacy, and the interconnectedness of all living beings.

The journey through this chapter is not merely speculative. Drawing from diverse fields such as philosophy, literature, spirituality, and science-focused exploration, it seeks to paint a holistic picture of what life might mean when freed from the finiteness of mortality. From ancient wisdom that revered the cyclical nature of life and death to futuristic projections of endless consciousness, we will traverse a tapestry of ideas that compel us to rethink the ultimate frontier of existence.

By the end of this chapter, readers will not only confront the profound implications of eternity but also find themselves questioning their own definitions of life and what it means to truly "live."

The Philosophical Recalibration: Eternity and the Meaning of Life

The concept of eternity fundamentally shifts how we understand the purpose and fulfilment of life. Traditional philosophy has long grappled with questions of finitude: What should one do with a life that is limited in time? How does the inevitability of death shape the value of our actions? Mortality has often served as the backdrop against which human ambitions, ethical decisions, and existential musings have been framed. However, when eternity becomes a conceivable reality, the thought-provoking landscape transforms dramatically.

One of the first challenges posed by the prospect of eternal life is the potential redefinition of purpose. In a finite existence, purpose is frequently tethered to the urgency of time—a race to achieve, contribute, and experience before the clock runs out. But in an eternal framework, the pressure to prioritize and optimize fades. Does this lead to a deeper, more intrinsic search for meaning, or does it breed complacency and ennui?

Fulfilment, too, may take on new dimensions. In a world where time is infinite, the milestones that once punctuated a life—graduation, career success, family, and personal achievements—could lose their gravity. Philosophers like Friedrich Nietzsche warned of the "eternal recurrence," where repetition might render all actions and experiences devoid of significance. Yet, others, like Alan Watts, have argued that endless existence could foster a greater appreciation for the present moment, as the fear of it slipping away dissipates.

Eternal life also challenges the ethical frameworks that underpin purpose. The idea of living forever forces us to confront questions about overpopulation, resource allocation, and the responsibility of immortals toward the planet and future generations. Should eternity compel us to adopt more sustainable, altruistic lifestyles, or will it intensify self-centeredness and apathy?

Furthermore, the notion of individuality undergoes profound shifts. If a person's essence persists indefinitely, how does one's identity evolve? Do we lose ourselves in the accumulation of endless memories, or do we find deeper self-knowledge over time? Philosophical traditions from Buddhism to existentialism offer differing perspectives—some suggesting that eternity might dissolve the ego, while others posit that it could amplify the quest for authentic selfhood.

The recalibration required to understand life through the lens of eternity is not merely intellectual. It demands an emotional and psychological adjustment to the absence of finitude. Would an eternal existence amplify our capacity for gratitude and wonder, or would it dull our sensitivity to life's fleeting beauties? The answers are as varied as the thought-provoking traditions that have explored these themes, but they all point to the need for a new paradigm of meaning, one that transcends the boundaries of mortality.

Eternity challenges us to rethink the foundations of purpose and fulfilment. It forces us to ask not just "What is the meaning of life?" but "What is the meaning of an infinite life?" As we move through this chapter, we will continue to explore how this recalibration impacts other facets of existence, from morality to relationships, and beyond.

Timeless Morality: Ethics in an Endless Existence

The advent of eternal life ushers in an era where ethical considerations must evolve to meet the demands of a society unbound by the constraints of mortality. Traditionally, moral systems have been shaped by the inevitability of death and the recognition of life's temporal limits. These frameworks often prioritize fairness, equality, and the distribution of resources within a finite timeline. In a world where life is unending, however, the ethical calculus transforms.

One of the most immediate challenges is the question of resource allocation. If individuals live indefinitely, how does society balance the needs of the eternal with those of the newly born? Overpopulation could strain ecosystems, exacerbate inequalities, and force a revaluation of what it means to live responsibly. A timeless existence might necessitate new ethical paradigms that emphasize sustainability, conservation, and a more profound respect for the planet's finite resources.

Eternal life also compels us to reconsider interpersonal right and wrong. How does one approach concepts like justice, forgiveness, and accountability when time itself is no longer a limiting factor?

In traditional societies, justice often carries a sense of finality, with punishments and redemptions framed within the boundaries of a mortal lifespan. In an immortal society, the permanence of consequences could either demand more leniency—allowing for endless opportunities for reform—or stricter accountability, given the potential for harm to persist indefinitely.

Furthermore, relationships take on new ethical dimensions. Love, loyalty, and commitment are often predicated on the understanding that life is fleeting. In an eternal world, do these bonds strengthen as individuals grow together over centuries, or do they fragment under the weight of endless time? Ethical frameworks may need to adapt to accommodate the fluidity and evolution of relationships in a timeless existence.

The right and wrong of innovation and progress also come under scrutiny. In a finite world, the rapid pace of technological advancement is often driven by the urgency of mortality. But in a timeless society, would the motivation to innovate wane? Or would the absence of time constraints enable a deeper, more thoughtful approach to problem-solving and creativity? The ethical implications of such shifts would ripple across industries, science-focused pursuits, and cultural development.

Finally, the moral responsibility of immortals toward future generations becomes a central question. Does eternal life grant individuals a greater duty to steward the planet for those yet to come? Or does it engender a sense of detachment, as the boundaries between present and future blur? Philosophical traditions, from the Native American concept of planning for seven generations to modern environmental right and wrong, offer valuable insights into how timeless morality might take shape.

The emergence of eternal existence demands a fundamental rethinking of right and wrong. It challenges humanity to craft new moral frameworks that prioritize sustainability, justice, and interconnectedness in an infinite timeline

Redefining Relationships: Love, Family, and Friendship in an Eternal World

Eternity transforms the very fabric of human relationships. Bonds formed under the premise of finite existence—where each moment is cherished for its fleeting nature—may evolve in profound ways when permanence becomes the norm. In an eternal world, love may deepen, becoming a continuous exploration of shared experiences, or it may face challenges from the monotony of endless familiarity.

Romantic relationships, in particular, would face both opportunities and challenges. Love, often strengthened by shared struggles and the awareness of time's limitations, might shift in an eternal existence. While some couples may use infinite time to explore new facets of their connection, rediscovering each other across centuries, others might struggle to maintain passion and novelty, risking stagnation or estrangement.

For families, the prospect of eternal life raises questions about generational dynamics. Will the absence of mortality blur traditional roles of parent, child, and elder? A parent might remain forever youthful alongside their offspring, complicating the natural cycle of caregiving and mentorship. Conversely, shared lifetimes could deepen familial bonds, offering unprecedented opportunities for collaboration, understanding, and collective memory-building.

Friendships, too, are likely to evolve. Lifelong friends might adapt and grow together, finding new ways to connect over centuries.

Alternatively, the vastness of time may lead individuals to drift apart, seeking fresh perspectives and new companionships. Long-term friendships could become as intricate as family trees, branching out and intertwining over eons.

New types of relationships might also emerge, forged by shared eternal experiences. Communities of immortals could foster bonds based on collective projects or goals that span millennia, reshaping the way individuals relate to one another. Ultimately, relationships in an eternal world would need to embrace flexibility, allowing for cycles of growth, transformation, and renewal while retaining a core of mutual respect and empathy.

The Legacy Paradox: Memory, Achievement, and Significance across Infinite Time

Legacy, for centuries, has been intertwined with the impermanence of human life—a testament to our fleeting existence and a desire to leave a mark on the world before we depart. The awareness of mortality has historically driven individuals to achieve greatness, build monuments, and create works that transcend their lifetimes. But what happens to the concept of legacy in a world where time is no longer finite?

In a reality unbound by the constraints of mortality, the very essence of legacy shifts. With infinite time to achieve, influence, and create, one must ask: Does the urgency to leave a mark diminish, as there are endless opportunities to do so? Or does it intensify, as individuals seek to craft works of such enduring brilliance that they stand out amidst an eternity of potential contributions?

Memory emerges as a critical dimension of this paradox. Human minds are not infinite in capacity, and over centuries or millennia, the accumulation of experiences and achievements may blur into an indistinct haze. Could the weight of endless time render past milestones insignificant, swallowed by the ever-growing tide of new endeavours? Or would it challenge individuals to cultivate selective memory, curating moments and achievements that define their enduring identity?

Furthermore, the paradox invites reflection on the interplay between individual and collective memory. In a world without end, will humanity's collective memory expand to honor countless legacies, or will it, too, be subject to the limitations of focus and priority? Could this lead to the erasure of once-profound contributions, or might it inspire new ways to preserve and celebrate the tapestry of human achievement?

As we delve into these profound questions, exploring whether infinite time renders legacy obsolete or reimagines it as an unending journey. In this context, legacy becomes less about finality and more about evolution—a continuous act of creation, influence, and contribution that seeks not just to endure but to resonate across the infinite canvas of existence.

Existential Risks and Eternal Lives: The Fragility of Infinity

Eternal life introduces profound vulnerabilities on both personal and societal levels, challenging our ability to adapt to a reality where time no longer defines human existence. On a personal level, the psychological toll of unending life may manifest in unexpected ways. Ennui—a deep, existential boredom—could arise as individuals exhaust novel experiences. Over time, despair might set in as they confront the overwhelming accumulation of memories, regrets, and an unrelenting passage of endless days. Identity crises may become common, as the evolution of self-identity across centuries can lead to a disconnection from one's former self, family, or culture. These psychological challenges threaten to erode the quality of eternal life, even as the body remains unyielding to time.

On a societal scale, the implications of living forever are equally daunting. Overpopulation becomes a stark inevitability in a world where people no longer die, leading to increased resource scarcity and environmental degradation. Even with advanced technologies to sustain resources, the strain on planetary ecosystems may reach catastrophic levels. Social hierarchies could harden, as living forever technologies, if accessible only to the privileged, widen the gap between the immortal elite and the mortal masses. This disparity could incite resentment, unrest, and ethical dilemmas, fracturing the very fabric of societies that living forever aims to preserve.

The preservation of an eternal society also hinges on navigating existential risks that, paradoxically, become magnified in the pursuit of living forever. Technological failures in life-extending systems could render entire populations vulnerable to sudden collapse. Catastrophic events—be they natural disasters, pandemics, or human-induced crises such as nuclear warfare—would gain new dimensions of severity in a world teeming with immortal beings. Furthermore, the stability of our planet is not guaranteed; climatic shifts, asteroid impacts, or other cosmic phenomena could threaten an eternal population concentrated on a fragile Earth.

These challenges demand a careful and collaborative approach to safeguarding eternal life. Innovative solutions must address overpopulation through space exploration, sustainable resource utilization, and ecological restoration. Psychological resilience could be bolstered through continuous mental health care, ethical counseling, and fostering a sense of purpose and meaning across eons.

At the same time, global frameworks must be established to ensure equitable access to living forever technologies, preventing them from becoming tools of division rather than progress.

The intricate balancing act required to sustain eternal lives, emphasizing that the pursuit of living forever is not merely a quest for technological advancement but a profound challenge to humanity's resilience, right and wrong, and collective ingenuity. The fragility of infinity reminds us that living forever, while alluring, requires thoughtful stewardship to ensure it enhances rather than imperils the human condition.

Cultural Reflections on Eternity: Insights from Literature, Art, and Religion

Throughout history, humanity has grappled with the idea of eternity through storytelling, art, and spirituality. From ancient myths of immortal gods to modern science fiction explorations of eternal consciousness, cultural expressions have served as mirrors to our deepest aspirations and anxieties about unending existence.

Religious traditions often frame eternity as a spiritual reward, contrasting the impermanence of temporal life with the promise of eternal bliss or enlightenment. Hinduism, for example, speaks of moksha—a liberation from the cycle of birth and death, merging the individual soul with the infinite divine. Christianity envisions eternity as a divine union with God, a state of everlasting peace and joy. Similarly, Buddhist philosophy contemplates eternity through the lens of nirvana, transcending suffering by dissolving the ego and embracing the timeless. These spiritual frameworks offer not only solace but also profound ethical guidance, shaping human behaviour with the promise of an eternal continuum.

Art and literature, on the other hand, often wrestle with the more ambiguous dimensions of eternity. From the tragic hubris of Greek figures like Tithonus, cursed with eternal life without eternal youth, to Mary Shelley's Frankenstein, exploring the moral perils of defying natural limits, stories have long warned of the burdens of living forever. In visual art, the Renaissance depictions of heaven and hell highlight the duality of eternal hope and eternal despair, offering a stark reminder of the moral weight tied to such an existence.

In modern times, science fiction has emerged as a key cultural lens to explore eternity, often portraying it as a technological achievement rather than a spiritual one. Works like Isaac Asimov's The Last Question ponder the intersection of eternal consciousness and cosmic evolution, while films like Inception and Interstellar probe the subjective experience of time and its potential to stretch into infinity. These narratives often juxtapose the promise of boundless existence with questions about the meaning of life when it is no longer finite.

Moreover, eternity often appears as a double-edged sword—an aspiration that reflects humanity's yearning for significance yet confronts us with the existential weight of endlessness. Would eternal life strip existence of urgency and meaning? Or would it open a boundless canvas for creativity, connection, and exploration?

As we delve into how diverse cultural lenses illuminate the multifaceted nature of eternity and its impact on human imagination, by reflecting on religious philosophies, artistic representations, and literary explorations, we uncover the profound ways in which eternity shapes our understanding of purpose, morality, and the human condition itself. It reveals that while the pursuit of eternity is as old as humanity, its implications continue to evolve, reflecting the dynamic interplay between our timeless hopes and contemporary realities.

The Role of Death in Giving Life Meaning: Does Immortality Diminish

Death has long been considered a defining feature of life, imparting urgency and significance to human actions. It is the shadow of our inevitable end that compels us to prioritize, cherish moments, and find purpose in our fleeting existence. But what happens when that shadow is removed? In a world without death, does life lose its meaning—or does it gain new dimensions of value and purpose?

Let us look into this profound question by exploring thought-provoking arguments on both sides, examining whether living forever enriches or erodes the human experience. It draws from existentialism, spirituality, and psychology to interrogate the relationship between mortality and meaning, questioning whether the absence of death redefines what it means to live fully.

Mortality as a Catalyst for Meaning

Existentialist thinkers such as Jean-Paul Sartre and Martin Heidegger argue that the finiteness of life is central to its value. Death, they contend, forces humans to confront the limits of their existence, sparking a quest for authenticity and purpose. Without the ticking clock, would we still strive to leave a legacy, love deeply, or pursue our passions with fervour? Heidegger's concept of "being-toward-death" emphasizes that the awareness of mortality is what makes life feel precious and urgent. From this perspective, living forever risks a numbing of the human spirit, potentially leading to complacency, boredom, and a loss of motivation.

Psychologically, the fear of death also shapes human behaviour. Terror Management Theory suggests that awareness of mortality drives cultural achievements, spiritual beliefs, and moral frameworks as a way to transcend the inevitability of death. If living forever were assured, would societies still feel the same drive to innovate, create, and explore?

The Case for New Horizons with Immortality:

On the other hand, advocates of living forever argue that removing the spectre of death could free humanity from fear, allowing for unprecedented exploration and growth. Instead of diminishing meaning, an eternal existence might enable individuals to continually reinvent themselves, cultivate long-term goals, and achieve deeper levels of understanding. In this view, life gains meaning not through its brevity but through the richness of its experiences, relationships, and contributions over time.

Spiritual perspectives often see living forever as an extension of the soul's journey. Ancient texts and philosophies, from the concept of moksha in Hinduism to the promise of eternal life in Christianity, reflect humanity's longing for transcendence. Would achieving living forever be the fulfilment of this longing, or a distortion of it?

The Paradox of Timelessness:

Immortality poses a paradox: while it may promise infinite opportunities, it could also dilute the value of individual moments. If time becomes unlimited, do we risk taking experiences for granted? The psychological principle of "scarcity value" suggests that rarity enhances appreciation—could an eternal life, devoid of scarcity, make joy, love, and achievement feel hollow?

Yet, there is also the possibility that human creativity and resilience could adapt to the new reality. Perhaps, instead of fearing an infinite timeline, we might learn to savour life's cycles in a deeper, more sustained way, finding purpose in creation, exploration, and the betterment of humanity.

Redefining the Human Experience:

The interplay between death and meaning is a central question of the human condition. Immortality challenges deeply ingrained assumptions about what it means to live a meaningful life. While the absence of death could risk eroding urgency and appreciation, it might also open new dimensions of purpose, creativity, and connection.

Ultimately, whether living forever diminishes or enhances value depends on how humans choose to navigate an existence without end. By examining the psychological, thought-provoking, and spiritual implications, we can better understand how mortality—and its absence—shapes the essence of being alive.

Unity through Eternity: Interconnectedness in an Immortal World

An eternal perspective reshapes the human experience, fostering a profound sense of interconnectedness that transcends the boundaries of time, space, and individual concerns. When mortality no longer dictates the urgency of our actions, humanity may come to recognize a shared destiny, one that emphasizes collective well-being, planetary stewardship, and the pursuit of a harmonious existence.

Immortality has the potential to dissolve the barriers between "self" and "other," as the continuity of life encourages individuals to consider the long-term implications of their actions. With infinite time at their disposal, people might shift their focus from fleeting, self-serving pursuits to the enduring impact they can have on the world around them. This paradigm shift could give rise to a culture that values collaboration over competition and prioritizes the flourishing of the collective over the desires of the individual.

The Collective Spirit in an Immortal Society:

In a society where lifespans stretch indefinitely, the concept of community takes on a transformative meaning. Time-intensive endeavours, such as resolving global conflicts, advancing science-focused understanding, or repairing ecological damage, would no longer feel constrained by the brevity of life. Instead, these efforts might be seen as shared, multigenerational projects where cooperation becomes indispensable.

Immortality could also inspire a revaluation of relationships, both personal and societal. With endless time to nurture connections, empathy and understanding might deepen, reducing prejudice and fostering inclusivity. Lifelong alliances, partnerships, and networks would carry the potential to grow ever stronger, bridging cultural, geographic, and ideological divides.

Planetary Stewardship and Cosmic Ambitions:

An immortal humanity might feel a heightened responsibility for Earth, recognizing it as a shared home that must be preserved for countless generations. This mindset could inspire a collective commitment to sustainable living, advanced ecological restoration, and a rebalancing of human impact on the planet. Stewardship of Earth could become not just a moral imperative but also a central purpose in a timeless society.

Moreover, living forever might fuel an unprecedented era of cosmic exploration. With limitless time, humanity could turn its gaze outward, embarking on long-term space missions and interstellar endeavours that were once deemed impractical. The stars could become the stage for a unified human race, united not just by biology but by shared purpose and vision.

A Purpose beyond the Self:

Eternal life offers the potential for an expanded sense of purpose, one that goes beyond individual achievements to encompass the broader arc of human progress. Art, philosophy, and science might flourish as individuals dedicate centuries, even millennia, to mastering their crafts or unraveling the mysteries of existence. Collective endeavours, such as mapping the universe or solving the deepest existential questions, could become humanity's shared legacy.

However, unity in an immortal world is not guaranteed. It will require deliberate effort, a reimagining of societal structures, and a commitment to values that prioritize the collective good. Only by embracing our interconnectedness and working together can we transform the challenges of eternity into opportunities for profound growth and harmony.

The author invites you to consider the possibilities of an immortal society, one where interconnectedness fosters unity, collaboration drives progress, and humanity embarks on a shared journey through time and space.

The Aesthetic of the Infinite: Beauty and Creation beyond Time

Art and beauty are often rooted in the ephemeral—a fleeting sunset, a momentary emotion, the transient brilliance of life itself. These are moments that touch the soul precisely because they are finite, reminders of the fragile, fleeting nature of existence. Yet, in an immortal world, the context of creation shifts dramatically. Without the boundaries of time, how does creativity evolve? Does it soar to unprecedented heights, liberated from the urgency of death, or does it stagnate in the endlessness of eternity?

In a world unshackled by the passage of time, the very motivations for artistic expression may transform. For centuries, art has been an attempt to capture the fleeting—a rebellion against the impermanence of life. Paintings, sculptures, music, and literature often strive to preserve beauty, emotion, or truth before they fade away. But in a realm where nothing fades, where memories are eternal and moments infinite, the question arises: What would be left to capture?

Artists might find inspiration in eternity, creating works of immense scale and unparalleled depth. Imagine cathedrals designed over millennia, symphonies spanning centuries, or novels that unfold across the ages. Free from the constraints of mortality, creativity could explore dimensions of beauty and fascination previously unimaginable. The infinite timeline could allow for perfectionism of a kind never before possible—each brushstroke refined, each note composed with meticulous care, each word chosen with deliberate precision. Such works could stand as timeless monuments to the endurance of human creativity.

Yet, there is a paradox. The absence of temporal limits could also stifle innovation. Deadlines often fuel invention; urgency is a catalyst for ingenuity. Without the ticking clock, would the fire of creativity dim? The abundance of time might lead to procrastination or a loss of urgency to create at all. When eternity stretches endlessly ahead, the value of the present moment can diminish, and with it, the intensity that often fuels artistic passion.

Moreover, the human capacity to appreciate beauty might evolve in unexpected ways. Would eternal existence desensitize us to awe? If sunsets became infinite, would they lose their magic? Or, conversely, would living forever expand our ability to perceive subtle nuances, enabling a deeper, more profound appreciation of the world around us?

On reflecting on the relationship between living forever, creativity, and the human capacity to appreciate beauty, living forever offers the promise of boundless creative potential but also poses profound questions about the nature of inspiration, the value of the ephemeral, and the role of beauty in shaping the human experience. In navigating eternity, humanity may discover that the aesthetic of the infinite is not about transcending time, but about learning to see the timeless in the fleeting moments we once took for granted.

Eternity and the Unknown: Embracing Mystery in the Face of Infinity

As we stand on the precipice of the unknown, imagining lives that stretch endlessly into the future, one thing becomes abundantly clear: mystery is eternal. Even in a world where death no longer looms as an inevitability, questions about the origins of the universe, the nature of consciousness, and the true boundaries of knowledge will persist. These are the enigmas that have stirred humanity's soul for millennia, urging us to explore, question, and seek meaning.

Immortality, should it ever be achieved, will grant us unparalleled opportunities for exploration and discovery. Yet, it will not resolve every mystery, nor should it. The unknown is not an obstacle to be overcome; it is a vital element of the human experience. It fosters curiosity, fuels innovation, and nurtures the awe that connects us to something greater than ourselves.

Consider the night sky—its vast expanse littered with stars, each one a burning sun millions of light-years away. Even with our advancing technologies, the cosmos remains largely unexplored. What lies beyond the farthest reaches of our telescopes? What forces birthed the universe we inhabit? Such questions may never have definitive answers, and that is a gift. The infinite invites us to dream, to imagine, and to craft narratives that give life its texture and depth.

In embracing eternity, we must also embrace the humility it demands. Our growing mastery over nature and life may tempt us to believe we are omnipotent, but true wisdom lies in acknowledging our limitations. The mysteries that remain unsolved are not failures of human ingenuity but reminders of the boundless source of fascination on our existence.

As readers of this book, you have embarked on a journey through science, right and wrong, and the dreams of living forever. Together, we have explored the incredible potential of human ingenuity, the ethical dilemmas it engenders, and the profound implications for society and self. But as we reach the end of this exploration, we must remember that every answer we uncover gives rise to new questions.

Immortality, if it is ever within our grasp, will not strip us of our humanity. Instead, it may magnify it. Our capacity for awe, discovery, and growth will endure, perhaps even deepen, as we confront the infinite. We will continue to seek meaning, to create beauty, and to connect with one another in ways that transcend time.

In the end, it is not the prospect of eternal life that defines us, but how we choose to live in the face of the unknown.

So, dear reader, as I bid you farewell, carry with you this final thought: to live is to wonder, and to wonder is to be truly alive. Whether our days are numbered or infinite, let us preserve the mystery and marvel that make existence worthwhile. For in the embrace of the unknown, we find not only the essence of what it means to be human but also the promise of what we may yet become.

www.ingramcontent.com/pod-product-compliance
Lightning Source LLC
LaVergne TN
LVHW041148150826
845673LV00001B/100